Hermann Lueer

GREAT DEPRESSION 2.0
Arguments against Capitalism

Hermann Lueer

GREAT DEPRESSION 2.0

Arguments against Capitalism

© 2024 Hermann Lueer

herluee@yahoo.com

Red & Black Books

Bordesholmer Straße 22

22143 Hamburg, Germany

ISBN 9798647961518

First release in German 2016

»Das Gespenst der Deflation geht um«

»Capital itself is the processing contradiction in that it seeks to reduce working time to a minimum, while on the other hand it sets working time as the only measure and source of wealth.«

Karl Marx

Preface

*"The process ... that incessantly revolutionizes the economic
structure from within, incessantly destroying the old one, incessantly creating a new one, this process of Creative Destruction
is the essential fact about capitalism. ... The process as a
whole works incessantly in the sense that there always is either
revolution or absorption of the results of revolution, both together forming what are known as business cycles."* [1]

A superficial look at the major capitalist economic crises seems to confirm the *business cycle* picture.

1929 Great Depression

1970 First Energy Crisis

1979 Second Energy Crisis

1982 Latin American Debt Crisis

1990 Japanese Asset Price Bubble

1997 Asian Financial Crisis

2001 New Economy Crisis

2008 Global Financial Crisis

---

[1] J. A. Schumpeter, Capitalism, Socialism, and Democracy, Second Edition Text, Impact Books 2014, Pos. 1899

A closer look at the various capitalist crises remains similarly superficial when the particularities of these crises are in the foreground.

In the face of the New Economy Crisis, for example, many people suddenly became interested in companies whose stock market value was supposedly far too high in relation to their turnover. During the global financial crisis, strange financial products like asset-backed securities suddenly became exciting topics, as did the question of whether it was right to bail out the banks. The common cause of all these capitalist crises was only marginally addressed, if at all. There is a widespread tendency to deal with the circumstances of the crisis rather than to explain them.

As long as the general nature of these capitalist crises, their common cause, is not clarified, neither their peculiarities nor their connections can be understood. *Those who do not want to deal with capitalism will not understand its crises.* Those who only scratch the surface of each crisis will not be able to understand how these crises come about and what political-economic connections exist between them.

In what follows, therefore, the question of the cause of capitalist crises will be posed. On this basis, it will be shown that the great capitalist crises of the past decades are neither isolated crises nor an economic cycle, but rather an *evolving contradiction* of capitalist production. At the same time, it will become clear why there can be no return to the *"golden age of capitalism"* and why the struggle against the dominance of finance capital, which is widespread among both left and right critics of the crisis policies, does not counteract the development of more extensive and more destructive crises.

Closed due to
overproduction

1. The phenomenon of capitalist economic crises

"Capitalism is admittedly not the only production relationship in which, in addition to immense wealth, there is also immense poverty. But it is the only mode of production where the abundance of goods is a problem. Where too much wealth is the ruin of society." [2]

The capitalist economic crisis is a strange crisis! All the material wealth and means of production are still available and yet the impoverishment of the population is growing to the point of mass pauperization. There has been no fire, no drought, no flood and no earthquake. The material wealth of society has not been destroyed by a natural disaster. There was not too little production, but too much. There is not too little productive potential, but overcapacity.

Overcapacity - too much wealth - is the phenomenon of capitalist economic crises.

This phenomenon has been observed in countries such as Greece, Spain and the U.S. in the wake of the global financial crisis. In the U.S. and Spain, there were

---

[2] Michael Heinrich, An Introduction to the Three Volumes of Karl Marx's Capital, 2012, p. 169

suddenly too many houses everywhere. Not because nobody wanted to live in them. On the contrary! Houses were forcibly evacuated on a large scale and auctioned off. There were functioning health care systems - in Greece, for example - where the existing medical care for the population was dismantled and the doctors fired. Nor were factories and machinery destroyed. There were too many for capitalist production. Millions of people became unemployed and destitute, even though they wanted to work. According to official figures from the International Labor Organization (ILO), unemployment rose by 30 million to a total of 200 million people worldwide as a result of the global financial crisis.[3] At the same time, factory occupations were outlawed. Occupied factories where workers wanted to continue working were forcibly evacuated by the police or military.

This apparent insanity - overcapacity alongside increasing mass impoverishment - is no secret to anyone. In the U.S., where millions have lost their jobs and their income, where millions of homes have been sold at foreclosure auctions, where the tent cities of the homeless were growing again, President Obama

---

[3] http://www.ilo.org/global/about-the-ilo/news-room/news/WCMS_202320/lang--en/index.htm

announced at the beginning of the global financial crisis:

"Our workers are no less productive than when this crisis began. Our minds are no less inventive, our goods and services no less needed than they were last week, or last month, or last year. Our capacity remains undiminished." [4]

So it could go on as before. All the physical means of production are still there, as are the workers and their willingness to work, not to mention the needs of the people. But then what is the reason for the crisis?

The bourgeois science gives the following reason, for example, the Nobel prize-winning economist Paul Krugman:

"Insufficient private spending to make use of the available productive capacity have become the clear and present limitation on prosperity for a large part of the world." [5]

Or Professor Rudolf Hickel, an academic advisor to Attac:

---

[4] Barack Obamas Inaugural Address,
https://obamawhitehouse.archives.gov/realitycheck/the_press_office/President_Barack_Obamas_Inaugural_Address
[5] Paul Krugman, The return of the depression economy and the crisis of 2008, p 182

"We have good production capacities, but they are not being used. What is missing is demand." [6]

The phenomenon of capitalist crisis seems crazy: An economic crisis because people don't want anything? Where are the needs in the crisis?

So the question arises: Is this crazy, or is the market economy not about satisfying the needs of the population? What is this strange wealth that - although the material conditions of production have not changed - is suddenly no longer available to a large part of the population? What is the yardstick of the market economy, what is the purpose of using the means of production?

The answer is no secret to anyone: the purpose that determines the capitalist mode of production is profit, based on privatized means of production. Of course, the professors also know that in the capitalist crisis there is not simply a lack of demand, but a lack of solvent demand.

---

[6] Junge Welt, 11.5.2013, S.8

Actually - one might think - there should be a revolt against the private appropriation of the means of production for the purpose of individual enrichment. After all, this is the reason for the exclusion and impoverishment of large sections of the population, despite the existing wealth of society, which is deplored as overcapacity.

So the question is: why does this not upset the majority of the population? Given the unpleasant consequences of capitalism, which everyone knows, how is it possible to have an unshakeable faith in the market and its sacred cow, the private ownership of the means of production?

The key word is *market failure*. The error of this conception is that it does not determine what the capitalist mode of production and the market are in order to draw the necessary conclusions, but, conversely, that the unpleasant consequences are interpreted as a failure of what the capitalist mode of production and the market *should be*.

In practical life, the consensus is that it makes no sense to pursue a goal by pursuing an end that is contrary to the goal. In this sense, it would be utterly nonsensical to believe that the owners of the means of production would ensure the prosperity of all by pursuing the goal of private enrichment. And yet that is precisely the idea of the defenders of capitalism. Suddenly, this idea - market failure - makes market competition seem to have the purpose of "providing for the good of all," against which it fails if not properly regulated.

This idea is widespread: From neoliberals, who want the market to regulate itself, to market socialists, who want the market largely regulated by the state. Thus, in the face of the capitalist crisis it is irresponsible speculators and greedy bank managers, or the lack of regulation by the state, who stand for the idea of "market failure".

In contrast the following will show why the well-known unattractive side effects of capitalism are by no means market failures, but rather the necessary consequences of the capitalist mode of production, and why they cannot be eliminated at all by regulatory measures.

2. The purpose and measure of capitalist production

If you look up what capitalism or a market economy is, you will find the following definitions, for example, in Wikipedia:

> *"Capitalism is an economic system based on the private ownership of the means of production and their operation for profit. In a capitalist market economy, decision-making and investments are determined by every owner of wealth, property or production ability in financial and capital markets whereas prices and the distribution of goods and services are mainly determined by competition in goods and services markets."* [7]

And as for the market economy:

> *"A market economy is an economic system in which the decisions regarding investment, production and distribution are guided by the price signals created by the forces of supply and demand. The major characteristic of a market economy is the existence of factor markets that play a dominant role in the allocation of capital and the factors of production."* [8]

In the market economy or capitalism, the economic relations of the members of society do not consist in

---

[7] https://en.wikipedia.org/wiki/Capitalism, Mai 2020
[8] https://en.wikipedia.org/wiki/Market_economy, Mai 2020

the planned production and distribution of useful things on the basis of common means of production. In a market economy, *private labor and exchange*, rather than *collectively planned production*, determine the economic relations of the members of society. Here, the division of labor is organized in the contradictory form of independent private producers who enter into a social context only after production on the market. It is only in retrospect that the sale of their commodities reveals whether they have produced for society. If their commodities remain unsaleable, not only their product but also their work proves to be socially useless. The legal institution of private ownership of the means of production, i.e. the possibility of privatizing land and the means of production, establishes this contradictory form of social division of labor, in which it is not the cooperation of the members of society, but the competition for private economic success on the commodity markets that determines the form and content of the social relations of production.

Ownership of the means of production and trade in commodities also existed in pre-capitalist relations of production, but not in a form that was imposed on all spheres of social life. Only after the bourgeois revolutions, when freedom and equality of the person and the right to own the means of production were granted, did production become commodity production in all its scope, depth and breadth. It was only on this basis that all products were transformed into commodities, including the labor power of those members of society who had no other means of production.

Liberation from slavery and serfdom, combined with exclusion from the privatized means of production and the food and consumer goods produced by them in private ownership, meant for the majority of members of society both the possibility and the obligation to sell their labor power. As sellers of their labor power, the working population is granted freedom and equality, but not the means to live. These belong to the legitimate owners of the means of production. The free and equal citizens, who are at the same time without the means of production, are thus faced with the following choice: they take the liberty of not selling their labor power and remain destitute, or they try in all freedom to sell their labor power to a factory owner or landlord in order to obtain bread and butter and shelter. Marx and Engels described this situation almost 150 years ago as follows:

"a class of laborers, who live only so long as they find work, and who find work only so long as their labor increases capital.

These laborers, who must sell themselves piecemeal, are a commodity, like every other article of commerce ..." [9]

The guarantee of freedom and equality, as the overcoming of slavery and serfdom, means, without the simultaneous socialization of the means of production for the majority of the population, the remaining economic dependence on the private profit calculation of the minority of owners of the means of production. Exploitation - the forced use of other people's labor for private gain - is merely transformed from the open relationship of violence of earlier times into an objectified relationship between buyer and seller of the commodity of labor power. The extensive appropriation of social wealth in the hands of a minority no longer appears as the exploitation of other people's labor, but as labor paid for in wages.

In reality, however, the owners of the means of production do not buy labor, but labor power. Since labor power can create more value than is paid to workers competing for jobs in labor markets, the purchase of labor power becomes a means of enrichment for those who, for whatever reason, have enough money. When selling their commodities, buyers of labor simply use the difference between the value of the labor power

---

[9] Karl Marx and Frederick Engels, Manifesto of the Communist Party   https://www.marxists.org/archive/marx/works/download/pdf/Manifesto.pdf, p. 18

they buy on the labor market and the value the labor adds in production. Money thus becomes capital, the means to make more money out of money. Accordingly, the owner of money becomes a capitalist when he buys labor power and makes the worker work in order to increase his wealth.

The purpose that determines capitalist production is the accumulation of money as capital - not to obtain a certain sum of money, but as a self-serving process of constant increase of the capital employed. Wealth measured in money, in the abstract quantity of economic power of disposal, is excessive. This excess is not individual insanity. The organization of the social process of production as a competition between the owners of the means of production leads to the factual necessity of making the hunt for the increase of capital the purpose of one's own actions. Those who are not profitable enough in comparison with their competitors, those who fail to ensure favorable production conditions in time by laying off workers and intensifying work, cannot displace their competitors by expanding their capacities, but on the contrary run the risk of being displaced by the successful growth of their competitors.

The competition for market share is never-ending, and so is the drive to reduce unit labor costs. Each success is the starting point for the next round of competition.

For wage earners, this means increased competition for existing jobs. In the global competition between companies, the reduction of wage costs becomes a constraint, which at the same time limits the feasibility of all subsequent social policy measures due to the competition between nations.

Those who, on the basis of the liberal property system, have no means of production at their disposal and therefore have to sell their labor power on a daily basis, receive with their wages in the competition of job seekers on the labor market - as with any other commodity - on average the social reproduction value of their commodity, i.e. their labor power. Thus, even after the production process, after they have spent their wages on the means of subsistence and consumption customary in their economic environment, the workers have no means of production other than their labor power and must sell it again in order to obtain the means of subsistence. Thus, the capitalist process of production not only produces commodities and profit, but also produces and reproduces the capital relation itself, on the one hand the capitalist, on the other the wage laborer.[10]

---

[10] Karl Marx, Capital Vol. 1, p. 403, https://www.marxists.org/archive/marx/works/download/pdf/Capital-Volume-I.pdf

Social
is what
creates
work

Under capitalism, the owners of the means of production inevitably become richer in proportion to the wealth created by society, and the workers become correspondingly poorer. But the fact that the growing wealth in capitalist society is unequally distributed is only the directly visible result of the capitalist mode of production. Moreover, profit-oriented production determines the content of production down to the smallest detail, both on the product side and on the labor side.

In the market economy, where goods and services are offered as commodities, the quality of the products of labor, as well as the working conditions under which labor is performed, are only means to the end of capital accumulation. The widespread notion that supply and demand in the market, with more or less regulation, would ensure the demand-oriented coordination of production and consumption, therefore misses the point. Demand is not to be confused with the needs of the members of society, but means nothing other than solvent demand. Those who, for whatever reason, are unable to pay for their needs do not count in a commodity-producing society. The supply of goods and services is in no way related to the quantity and quality of goods and services needed to satisfy the needs of the members of society. *What* useful things are produced, *for whom*, *where* and *how* they are produced, determines the criterion of saleability on the market. In the interplay of supply and demand, consumers thus accept their exclusion from things they cannot pay for and orient their needs according to their wallets, while suppliers serve the different levels of solvency in the sense of their profitable business with goods of all kinds; cheap and expensive, healthy and unhealthy. The subordination to the purpose of saleability controls, behind the backs of the producers, the use of all social potentials of production and determines which needs count. Because of this subordination, in the market economy social labor is provided for the most eccentric individual need, if the individual, for whatever reason, has the corresponding ability to pay. At the same time, social labor is invested in inferior consumer goods in order to take advantage of the low solvency of the majority of the population. Despite all the display of wealth, in capitalism it is not the needs in relation to the required labor time that are the measure of what, how much and how it is produced, but the availability of money is the measure of the extent to which needs are met, and the ability to multiply money is the measure of what is produced, for whom or if at all. Under capitalism, no worker can be employed who does not produce more than the amount of his wage. Without profit for the owner of

the means of production, all production is meaning-
less, regardless of the needs of the population and the
availability of the means of production.

3. Economic Miracle – Economic Crisis

Contrary to popular belief, capitalism is not the reason for the technological progress that has transformed the world over the past one hundred and fifty years. The *reason* is the human mind and the social division of labor. The capitalist mode of production is merely the *form* in which technological progress has been ruthlessly advanced against workers and nature for the private enrichment of the owners of the means of production. A form of social division of labor in which the existing means of production and existing needs are not a sufficient reason for the use of the means of production, in which production depends rather on whether the owners of the means of production expect a profitable business from the production of any useful thing in relation to the solvency of the members of society. A production relation in which too much wealth in relation to solvency becomes the reason for the impoverishment of society.

But why does overproduction always occur under capitalism? Why does economic activity fluctuate between boom and bust? Why is it suddenly no longer worthwhile for the majority of capitalists to produce?

The answer is quite simple: if under capitalism private owners only allow the means of production to be used when other members of society can pay for their needs, then additional solvency is the reason for the use of privatized means of production that lie fallow without this solvency. More available money and thus more ability to pay means more growth potential in the market economy, less money reduces the growth potential. Simply printing money and making it available to members of society to promote economic growth would be conceivable, but it is not a sustainable solution. If all members of the society have more money for the same amount of commodities, the owners of the commodities can simply demand more money for their commodities, i.e. the prices rise and the money is devalued. In a market economy, real economic growth occurs only when additional commodity values are created, which are matched by the additional ability to pay. The additional ability to pay, which is put into circulation to promote economic growth, must therefore be combined with the obligation to produce more commodity values. Only then does the additional ability to pay have the power to generate real economic growth instead of inflation.

The promise of payment expressed in the loan agreement is the decisive *magic bullet* in the market economy. Privatized means of production, which would lie idle without solvency, are set in motion by solvency derived from confidence in creditworthiness. With what is in principle an endless chain of promises to pay, a multitude of capitalist economic activities and assets can be generated for which there would have been no capitalist reason without the credited solvency. This process of "credit money creation", which is essential for capitalist growth, can be well illustrated by the example of a simple bank loan.[11]

Let's assume that A (a private household or a company) pays 100 in a bank account at an interest rate of, say, 5%. The bank records an asset of 100 on its assets side and at the same time records 105 as a liability to the depositor on the liabilities side of its balance sheet.

Bank

Cash 100	105 Liabilities
	5 Loss

---

[11] In order to illustrate the process of credit creation as simply as possible, the following does not include a precise presentation of the individual transactions via the balance sheet and income statement. Instead, the receivables and liabilities resulting from the lending business, including interest, are presented against each other in a simplified balance sheet.

Even with this simple credit relationship - the depositor lends his money to the bank and speculates that the bank will be able to repay his deposit with 5% interest - the assets of the society have doubled: the depositor has a claim of 105 against the bank (his 100 plus 5% interest), and the bank has additional liquidity of 100 in the cash box.

Now, for example, the Bank lends the 100 to B at a lending rate of 10%. The 100 in the bank's treasury are transformed into 110 claims on B by this loan transaction, and the bank makes a profit of 5 on the difference between the deposit and the loan interest.

Bank

Receivables 110	105 Liabilities
	5 Profit

In a loan transaction involving its own or third-party funds, the bank sells the right to use the third party's assets as if they were its own in exchange for interest. While A continues to hold its assets in the form of a receivable and the bank also records a receivable from B as an asset, B can now dispose of the money and use it, for example, to buy production equipment from C.

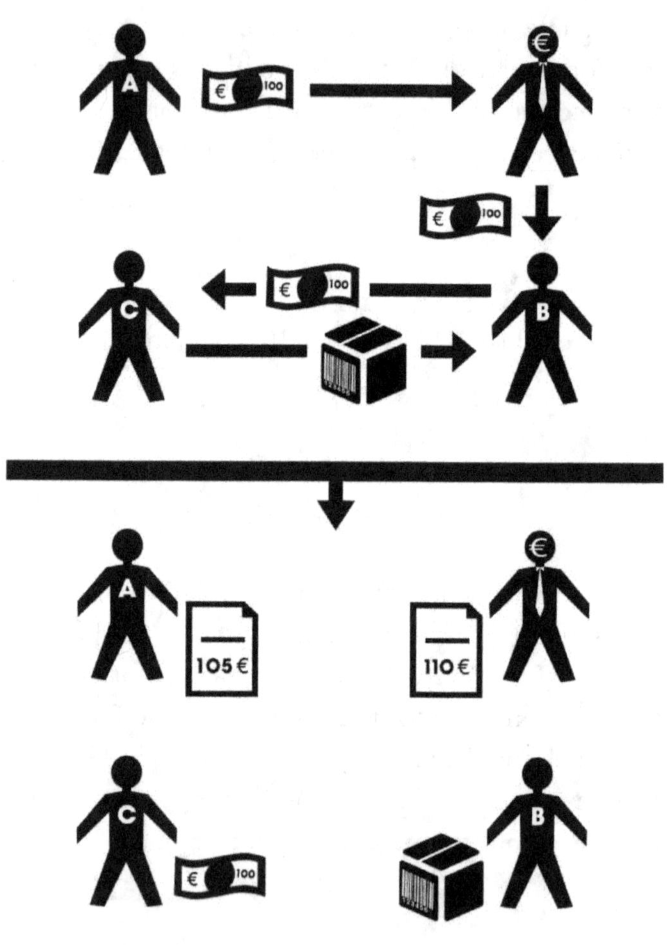

A
€ 100
€ 100
€ 100
C
B
105 €
110 €
€ 100

C now invests the money from the successful sale in a bank, the bank gives a loan to D, D buys from E, E invests his money in a bank, the bank gives a loan to F, and F buys from G.

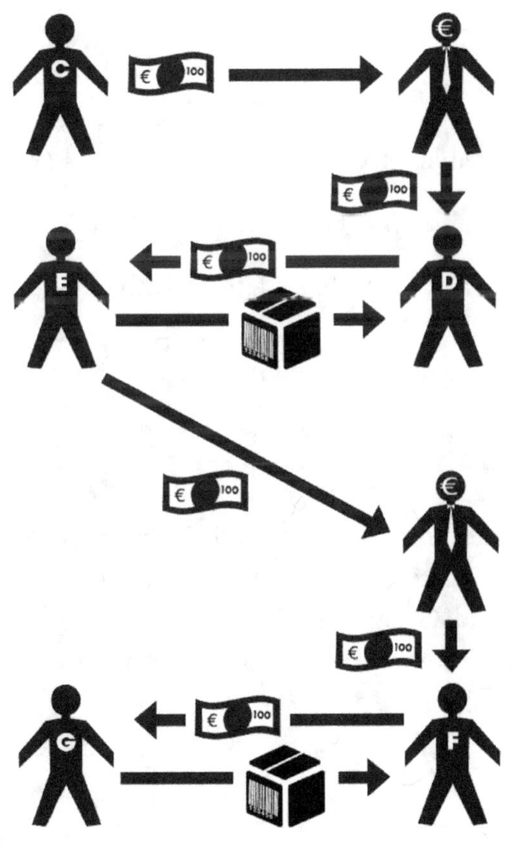

Starting from the 100 that A lent to a bank, the subsequent chain of credit multiplied the assets recorded, thus providing the basis for several transactions in the "real economy" for which the necessary solvency would not have been available without the chain of payment promises.

<table>
<tr><td colspan="2" align="center">Bank</td></tr>
<tr><td>Receivables (B) 110</td><td>105 Liabilities (A)</td></tr>
<tr><td>Receivables (D) 110</td><td>105 Liabilities (C)</td></tr>
<tr><td>Receivables (F) 110</td><td>105 Liabilities (E)</td></tr>
<tr><td></td><td>15 Profit</td></tr>
</table>

In parallel with the increased balance sheet total in the financial sector, A, C, and E each have 105 receivables, C, E, and G could sell their products, B, D, and F could consume or invest 100 each, and G has 100 in liquidity.

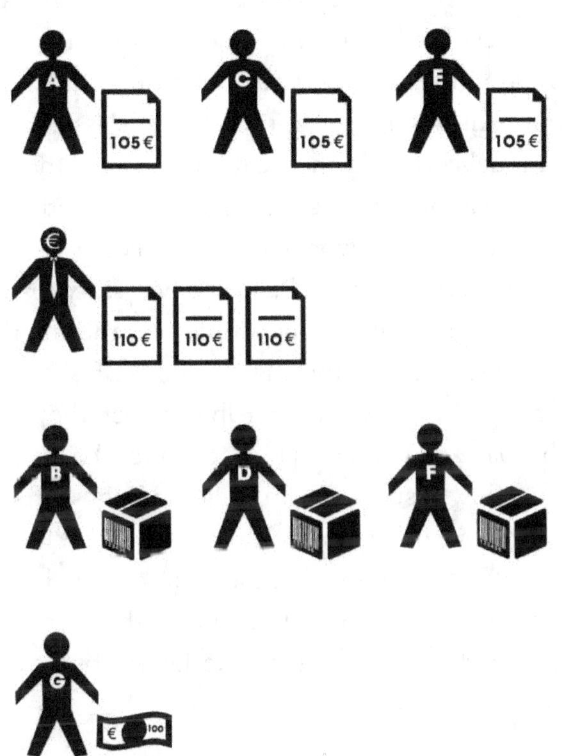

In the modern banking world, this credit money creation process is only marginally dependent on the monetary base in the form of customer deposits or other central bank reserves. Contrary to the classical multiplier model chosen in the example, in reality the credit money creation process works largely the other way round via the extensive interbank market: banks grant loans and subsequently obtain the necessary reserves. With its high liquidity and efficiency, the interbank market has become the main source of short-term funding for banks, with the help of which they generate the loan and the deposits that finance the loan. The cash outflow resulting from their lending is offset by borrowing, i.e. an increase in their debt. The limits of their lending are thus within the limits of their borrowing capacity and, in order to maintain their creditworthiness, within the limits of the bank's risk calculation.[12]

In addition to the creation of book money through lending, speculation on successful transactions on the capital market becomes the basis for issuing securities. Shares, bonds and derivatives derived from them are used to construct project- or company-related securities for a wide range of special interests. The special

---

[12] J. Ryan-Collins, Where does Money come from? New Economics Foundation 2012

feature of securities compared to loans is that the prospect of future earnings is turned into a saleable item. The issuer of securities creates additional capital by selling shares or corporate bonds to investors who invest in its future business success. The issuance of stocks and bonds converts debt into tradable financial capital for investors. At the same time, the money raised through the issuance of securities circulates in the economy in the context of the investments made with them and, similar to the multiplier model described above, becomes the basis for new loans and securities. As long as investors have confidence in the future success of companies, there are no limits to the issuance of securities and the extension of credit.

Under capitalism, privatized means of production lie idle, despite existing needs and willing workers, until they are set in motion by the prospect of money. Trust in the future solvency of the debtor, which is bindingly fixed in the credit or securities contract, becomes the means of growth. With the creditors' speculation on the success of the companies, the additional solvency necessary for its upswing is introduced into capitalist economic life via the loan or the securities. In this way, economic growth is generated, which would not be possible in capitalist terms without the solvency achieved through credit and securities, i.e. without the speculative expectation of a successful business or the income generated by it. In the capitalist mode of production, it is not the needs and labor capacities of the members of society that set the means of production in motion, but only the prospect of successful sales. Without credit, the baker or the engineer would have to wait for the return of the money from the successful sale before investing in the means of production again. Without the solvency anticipated by credit, there would indeed be sufficient means of production and labor to satisfy the needs of the population, but they would not have been used because the lack of solvency would simply have meant that the capitalist reason for their use would have been lacking.

This social madness - production is not determined by the needs and abilities of the members of society, but by the solvency available for profitable private business - does not remain without consequences. Not only in the growing gap between rich and poor, but also because of the capitalist crisis, in which suddenly too much wealth in relation to the existing solvency means the ruin of society. The contradiction that the workers must first earn money before they can buy, and that the employers will only invest in workers if there is a prospect of a successful sale for them, can be temporarily resolved in the sense of an upswing with the help of credit. Ultimately, however, the upswing that is fueled by the creation of credit stands and falls with confidence in future business. Speculation on future business success - which in the legal relationship between finance capital and the "real economy" is accounted for as if it had already occurred - must always prove to be real, albeit with a time lag, otherwise only the debts will actually grow, and the wealth they promise and record will become more and more illusory. If there is a generalized loss of confidence in future economic success, suddenly everyone wants to see money instead of credit, and since the equation in capitalism holds - without money there is no solvency, without solvency there is no business, without business prospects there is no production - even existing production capacities are shut down, and the impoverishment of the population grows along with overcapacities. This loss of confidence, which develops again and again on the basis of the individual assessment of business prospects, and thus the transition from economic miracle to economic crisis, receives its economic necessity from the following contradictions of capitalist production:

1. Capitalist competition for solvency creates overcapacity in relation to solvency.

In a market economy, a company's own market share should grow at the expense of its competitors. Regardless of the competition, everyone invests in their machines and in the expansion of their production facilities in order to increase their profits. In this competition, the size of capital is decisive. Those with fewer resources for research and development, an outdated machine park, lower economies of scale, a smaller marketing budget, or a less effective sales organization will soon be left holding the bag.

Access to credit therefore becomes the decisive competitive tool. Those who have access to credit can test the success of their business idea long before their competitors, who without credit have to save their start-up capital from daily living expenses. Those who, after producing commodities, have to wait for the return of their advanced money before they can invest again in raw materials and labor will lose market share to those who can bridge the normal circulation time of money through credit. Those who can finance expansion investments through credit can accelerate the growth of their business before sufficient profits have been accumulated.

In the competition for market share in which the capitalist economy is organized, companies therefore inevitably build up overcapacity compared to the available purchasing power by speculatively expanding their production capacities. And they do so not only with funds already generated by a successful business, but to a large extent with borrowed funds, speculating on their future success.

2. The source of profit - the exploitation of wage labor - is at the same time a cost factor deducted from profit.

The purpose that determines the capitalist mode of production is not to organize production according to a plan that takes into account the needs of the members of society. The share of the population in social production in the form of their wages is rather a cost factor in the profit calculation of the owners of the means of production, which determines their decision on production. Enterprises must constantly strive to reduce these costs in order to survive in the competition for the population's ability to pay. The reduction of wage costs and, consequently, the substitution of labor in the context of technical progress, reduces at the same time a part of the total economic demand for which the individual enterprises compete. The reason for the capitalist use of the means of production - the exploitation of the difference between the wages paid to the workers and the value added by their labor to the commodities produced - thus constantly comes into conflict with the condition of its realization: the solvency of the working population.

3. The greater the productivity of society, the less labor time it takes to produce a commodity, the lower the value of the commodity, which is the only thing that matters in capitalist production.

In capitalism, the satisfaction of the needs of the members of society is a means to the end of increasing the capital employed by the owners of the means of production. Expressed in terms of the wealth of capitalist society, this means that the exchange value of products is the end for which their use value is the means. Because of this dual character of products in capitalism, the development of productive forces is in constant conflict with their end, the increase of existing capital. If the socially established productivity increases, the value of the now more productively manufactured products decreases in relation to the socially necessary working time. Or as Karl Marx put it:

"The same change in productive power, which increases the fruitfulness of labor, and, in consequence, the quantity of use values produced by that labor, will diminish the total value of this increased quantity of use values, provided such change shorten the total labor time necessary for their production; and vice versâ." [13]

---

[13] Karl Marx Capital Vol. 1, SECTION 2, The two-fold character of the labor embodied in commodities, https://www.marxists.org/archive/marx/works/1867-c1/ch01.htm#S1

In other words, when socially necessary production costs are reduced as a result of competition-driven productivity gains, firms simultaneously reduce their sales and the associated profits. What would increase the wealth of society on the basis of the common means of production - a product can be produced with half the working time - reduces the social wealth in relation to the measure of capitalist production. This specifically capitalist contradiction - the measures to increase the growth of capital reduce it at the same time - can only be compensated by constantly increasing the production of goods. For example, if a socially enforced increase in productivity halves the value of a car, two cars will have to be sold in the future to realize the same value. If productivity is doubled at the same level, four cars must be produced and sold in the future to prevent a decline in sales. The additional product output must grow exponentially in relation to a given increase in productivity in order to prevent the shrinkage of the mass of value, which is the decisive measure of capitalist production. The development of the productive forces, which is a blessing based on the common means of production, is therefore a curse for many members of society within the framework of the capitalist mode of production.

In terms of the purpose of capital accumulation, less necessary work does not mean the same standard of living with more leisure time, but less ability to pay for those who have been laid off. At the same time, prices, and thus the volume of business, will fall once the productivity advantage among competitors has become generalized. Capitalist enterprises therefore have to grow, and this compulsion to grow means that enterprises constantly push the contradiction of capitalist production.

This contradiction is given its particular force by the lever of credit, i.e. by the effect of the creation of money and capital, which promotes the upswing and takes its necessary course in the alternation of boom and crisis. The solvency extended by the financial sector in its business interests, which in the course of the

---

[14] http://www.zeit.de/2008/43/Autobauer-Absturz

upswing enables capitalist enterprises as well as private households to operate with greater monetary power than they have brought about themselves, is withdrawn or devalued with the loss of confidence in business success just as massively as it originally came into the world through the granting of credit. Instead of investment in expansion and new hiring, there are now layoffs and bankruptcies. The sellers of labor power must realize that it is not their performance but the business calculations of their employers that matter. Insolvent needs degenerate into mere needs that are of no interest to anyone in capitalism. In addition, there are the functioning factories and machines and the unemployed people who would work but are not needed by the owners of the means of production because the use of their labor power is not worthwhile for them at the moment.

The uncontrolled effect of the formation and bursting of the credit bubble is supposed to be prevented by the state through its monetary, fiscal and foreign trade policies. However, over-production is not the result of misguided economic policies, but a necessary consequence of the capitalist mode of production. Whether competing firms use their rationalization efforts to deprive themselves of the necessary purchasing power, or whether, in parallel with their rationalization efforts, they use credit to expand their production capacities beyond the existing solvency of society, is ultimately irrelevant. The expansion of the economy, which is driven by everyone in their business interests against each other, inevitably reaches the limits of solvency at some point. Neither low interest rates nor consumer credit granted in the interest of the economy will change this.

In the capitalist mode of production, in which it is not the needs of the individual and not the existence of the means of production that are decisive for the owners of the means of production, but the individual ability to pay and the prospect of a profitable business, the creation of money in speculation on future business generates so-called "economic miracles", and the destruction of money accordingly leads to an "economic crisis", in which overcapacities are confronted with increasing poverty of the population.

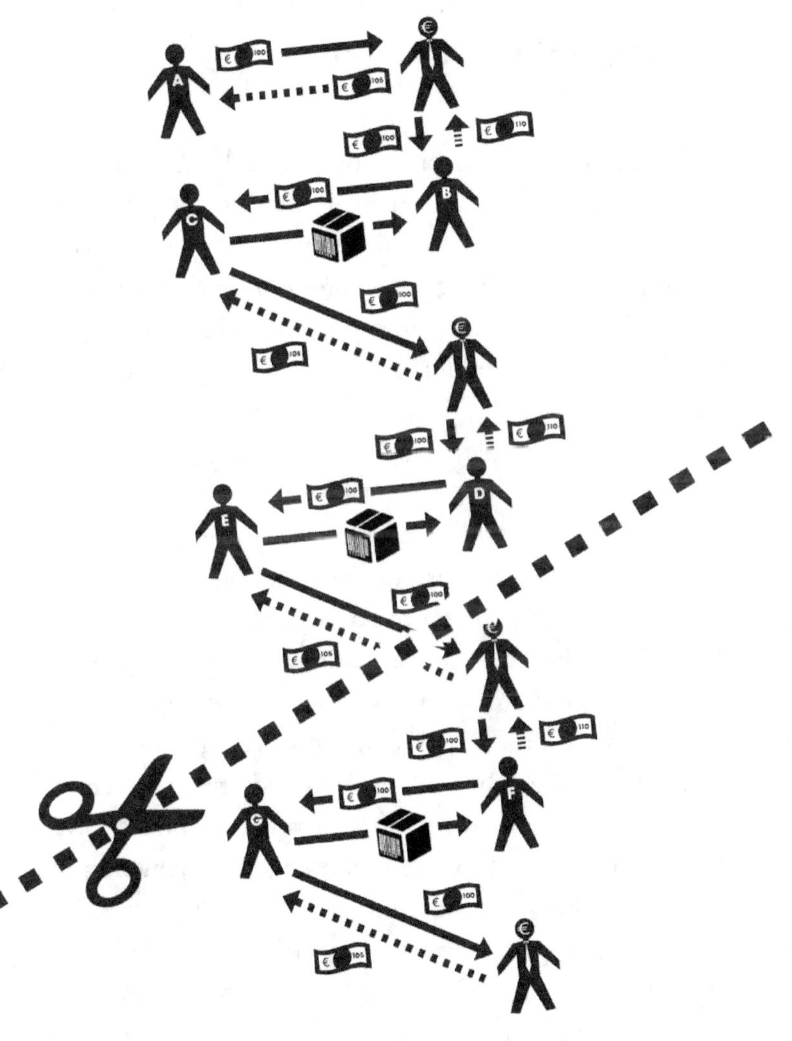

A
B
C
D
E
F
G

4. The evolving contradiction of capitalist production

The great economic crises of recent decades are not independent capitalist crises. Rather, in their specific form and in the economic policy attempts to overcome them, they are *the expression of the evolving contradiction* of capitalist production. As shown in the previous section, this contradiction, which develops over the cycles of boom and crisis, consists in the fact that, in the competition for available purchasing power, capital seeks to reduce unit labor costs by increasing productivity, while at the same time the purpose of capital accumulation is based on exploiting the ability to pay of the members of society. This contradiction, which is driven by the competition for cost leadership and market share - making labor superfluous on the one hand in order to exploit the solvency of the population on the other - is given an additional dynamic by the value-immanent contradiction of capitalist production: the need to compensate for the reduction in value resulting from the increase in productivity with additional growth. How this contradiction of capitalist production has developed in the course of technical progress, and how politicians try to cope with the necessary consequences by means of ever more credit - i.e. ever greater anticipation of future income - can be

well illustrated by the example of the USA as the dom-
inant capitalist market.

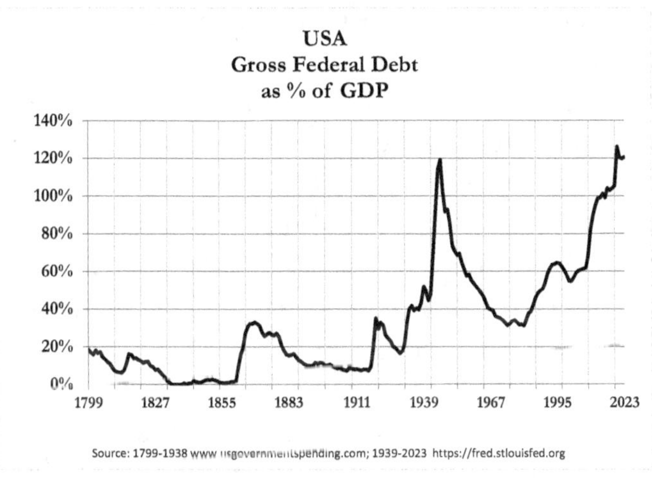

Source: 1799-1938 www.usgovernmentspending.com; 1939-2023 https://fred.stlouisfed.org

For the first 150 years of capitalist development, the
U.S. national debt was essentially tied to the financing
of wars. Beginning with the War of Independence
(1790), through the U.S. Civil War (1861-65), to U.S.
participation in World Wars I and II (1917/1941), the
government's borrowing requirements rose sharply
with the outbreak of war, but were largely reduced relative to economic growth after the wars ended. Even
after the Second World War, the ratio of gross federal
debt to GDP fell for more than three decades to just
below the pre-war level. From 1980 onwards, the ratio

rose from 30% to a new level of around 60% and, following the global financial crisis, has reached a level of 120% of economic output. Critics of so-called neoliberalism argue that the period from 1980 onwards, initiated by Ronald Reagan in the U.S. and Margaret Thatcher in Europe, was a failure of policy. As a "change of course from social Keynesianism to the doctrines of a radical market formation of society" that should and supposedly could be reversed. That this idea of a return to the supposed *"golden age of capitalism"* is unrealistic, and where developments are heading instead, becomes clear as soon as one takes a closer look at the reasons for the changes in the direction of economic policy in the last century. To this end, we take the example of the U.S. gross federal debt to examine the three decades of Keynesian economic policy before the change of course in the early 1980s.

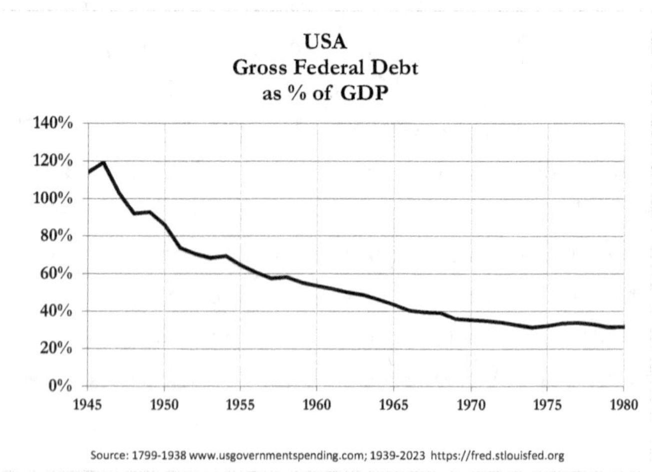

Source: 1799-1938 www.usgovernmentspending.com; 1939-2023 https://fred.stlouisfed.org

During three and a half decades of Keynesian economic policy, the high level of debt left over from the Second World War fell from 119% to less than 35% of GDP by the end of the 1960s, thanks to average economic growth of 4%, and seemed to stabilise at this level in relation to economic output. Two factors were responsible for this development.

On the economic side, the long-lasting economic upswing, which led to a reduction in relative debt, was supported by scientific and technical progress, which in the second industrial revolution from the end of the 19th century to the middle of the 20th century was made possible by a large number of decisive inventions. From household appliances, medical technology and consumer electronics to the automotive and aerospace industries, mass production was achieved on the basis of fundamental inventions using new materials and production processes, enabling enormous market expansion through the development of entirely new markets. An economic revolution that cannot be repeated in this form, since its achievements can only occur once as an innovation. In this phase, the value- and thus growth-reducing effect of the productivity increase was successfully overcompensated by the expanded production in the newly created economic sectors. A situation that steadily lost its compensatory power as new market potentials were increasingly exploited. While growth rates averaged 4.5% in the 1950s, they approached the 2% mark by the end of the 1970s.[15]

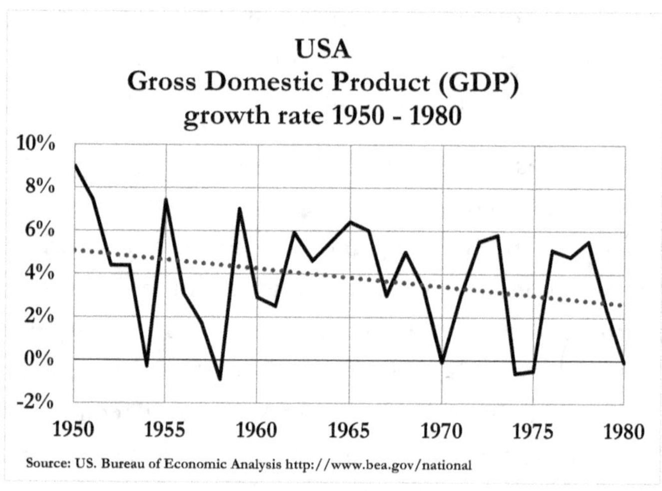

The second issue that played an important role in the background is political. At the end of the Second World War, the new international monetary order was agreed at Bretton Woods, with the abolition of the gold standard and the introduction of the U.S. dollar as a reserve currency (though initially with gold convertibility). In practice, this meant that the dollar, ac-

---

[15] Cf. Robert J. Gordon, The rise and fall of American growth, Princeton University Press 2016

cepted as the world's money, allowed the U.S. to finance global economic growth by issuing its own currency. On this basis, the Keynesian policy of growth-promoting public debt led to increased tax revenues which, as long as the economy grew, were reflected in an increase in absolute debt but not in relative debt. During this period, the government's expansion of the entire transportation infrastructure, various welfare state measures in the areas of education and medicine appropriate to a modern industrial workforce, as well as the escalating costs of the Vietnam War, could be financed through the worldwide sale of U.S. government bonds, even at the cost of a slight depreciation of the U.S. dollar. As early as the 1960s, the nominal value of U.S. dollars held by Europe and Japan exceeded U.S. gold reserves as a result of extensive government spending.

In 1971, the first loss of confidence in the gold convertibility of the U.S. dollar occurred in connection with rising U.S. trade deficits. The U.S. government's response was simply to remove gold convertibility and thus the limit on its national debt. As a result, the dollar continued to lose value. Whereas in 1971 the U.S. dollar was worth DM 3.49, by 1979 it had fallen to DM 1.18. In parallel with the devaluation of the U.S. currency, the compensation mechanism that had made it possible to increase the value of production during the second industrial revolution despite rising productivity slowed down. As a result, it became increasingly difficult during this phase to compensate for the redundancy of labor in the course of productivity progress by additional production in other, newly emerging sectors of the economy. Unemployment, i.e. the lack of opportunities to use labor profitably, rose to a level of 7% in the U.S. By 1973, the production capacities built up in the competition for solvency turned out to be overcapacities in relation to the available purchasing power. In this situation, OPEC's decision to raise oil prices triggered the first and second oil price crises. At the same time, the sharp rise in oil prices, the diminishing effect of growth-promoting public debt and the devaluation of the U.S. dollar led to rising inflation in the U.S. domestic market.

By 1980, inflation in the US had reached 14%. The coincidence of unemployment and inflation gave rise to a new economic term: stagflation - high unemployment combined with high inflation and low growth.

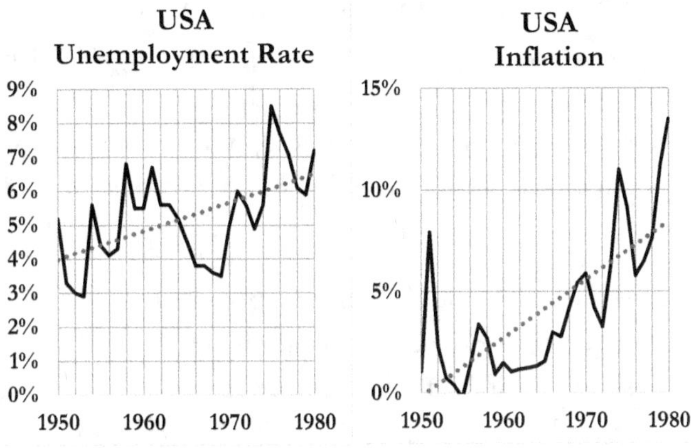

Source: Federal Reserve Economic Data, https://research.stlouisfed.org/

By the end of the 1970s, as rising inflation and unemployment made it clear that the attempt to stimulate aggregate demand for goods and services was failing, Keynesian economic policy became increasingly defensive. In their place, so-called neoliberal economic policies gained ground in the U.S. under Ronald Reagan and in Europe under Margaret Thatcher. In the explicit recognition that investment behavior and thus economic growth and employment are primarily determined by the profit expectations of entrepreneurs, the contradictions of capitalist production were to be overcome by improving capitalist business conditions within the framework of a supply-side economic policy. The "Program of Economic Recovery" adopted under Ronald Reagan put the following key

points on the economic policy agenda for this purpose: 1. the reduction of inflation by controlling the
growth of the money supply, 2. the reduction of tax
rates on capital and labor income, 3. the deregulation
of markets, and 4. the reduction of government spending.

The results of the new economic policy, implemented
over three presidential terms under Ronald Reagan
and his deputy and later successor George H. W. Bush,
were initially quite successful. The "stagflation" that
characterized the U.S. economy at the end of the
Keynesian economic era was overcome within a few
years of supply-side economic policies. A year before
Reagan took office, the new chairman of the Federal
Reserve, Paul Volcker, had already raised the federal
funds rate to 20%. The increase in the cost of credit
reduced the solvency of economic entities and many
previously promising business activities were discon-
tinued. Inflation fell from just under 14% to a new
level below 4% during the recession that began with
the increased cost of credit. At the same time that interest rates were rising, the top income tax rate was cut
in several steps from 70% to 28% and the corporate
tax rate was cut from 48% to 34% when Roland
Reagan took office to stimulate the economy. Unemployment, which rose sharply to 10% with the economic downturn at the beginning of Ronald Reagan's

presidency, was almost halved as the economy grew from 1983, but rose again to 8% with the economic crisis in 1991. Overall, the U.S. economy grew by an average of 3% over the three terms of "Reaganomics," despite the two economic downturns in 1982 and 1991.

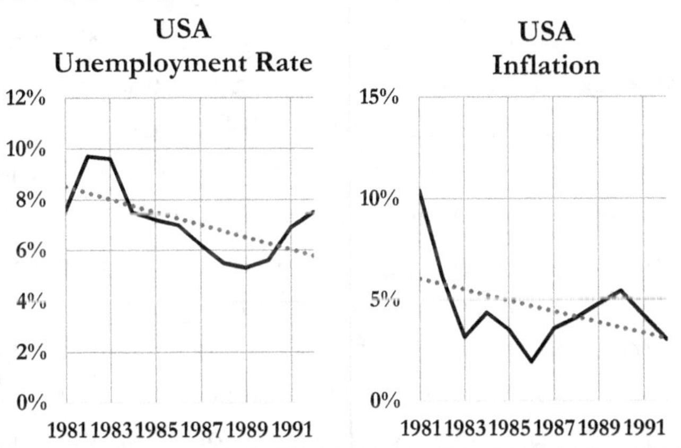

Source: Federal Reserve Economic Data, https://research.stlouisfed.org/

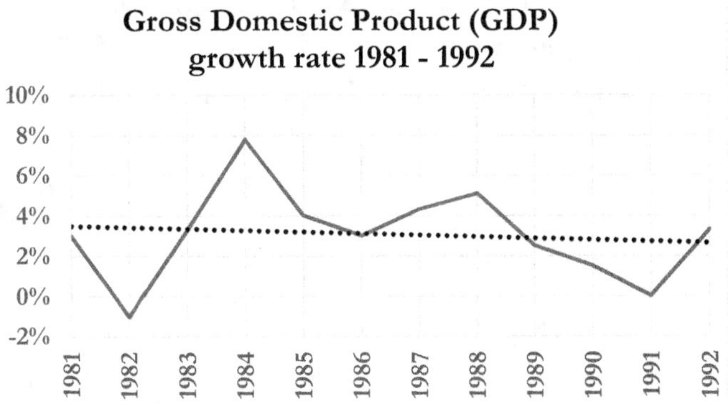

Source: US. Bureau of Economic Analysis, http://www.bea.gov/national/.

However, the stabilized capitalist economic development compared to the "stagflation" at the end of the Keynesian economic epoch is not only the result of the supply-oriented improvement of capitalist business conditions. In addition to the temporary stimulating effects, the improved economic situation was also the result of a gigantic increase in debt. The annual budget deficits, through which additional funds were regularly made available for economic stimulus under the Keynesian economic policy, rose from 70 billion U.S. dollars to 290 billion U.S. dollars during the Reagan and Bush administrations. The national debt as a percentage of gross domestic product rose from 30% to 60% during the three terms. Like a classic stimulus program, increasing debt-financed spending created income and employment that would have had no capitalist rationale without the debt. By speculating on future incomes, the budget deficits from 1981 to 1992 added an average of $190 billion a year in purchasing power, which was a not insignificant factor in the relative stabilization of U.S. capitalist production.

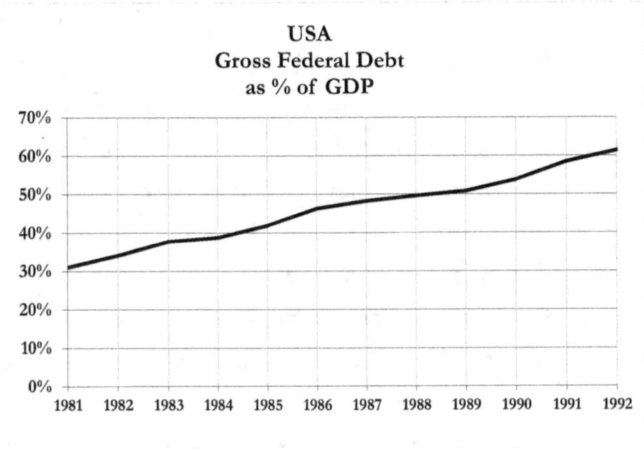

Source: 1799-1938 www.usgovernmentspending.com; 1939-2023 https://fred.stlouisfed.org

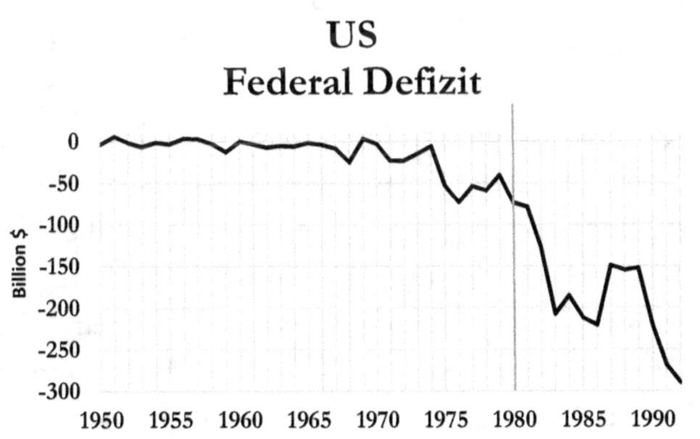

Source: Federal Reserve Economic Data
http://research.stlouisfed.org/fred2

The economic development from 1945 to the early 1990s shows that the contradictions of capitalist production cannot be resolved by either a demand-oriented or a supply-oriented economic policy. Demand-oriented economic policy, which is based on increasing purchasing power, has basically two starting points: First, it can take the form of credit-financed demand, directly creating the solvency necessary for capitalist growth through additional government spending, or indirectly creating incentives for additional borrowing by lowering interest rates. Second, it can contribute to an increase in purchasing power by redistributing income through taxes or direct wage increases. In the first case, demand-pull policy promotes inflation in parallel with output expansion by allowing producers to raise prices. In the second case, it accelerates the point at which the capitalist tendency toward "overproduction" leads to crisis. This is because if the additional purchasing power generated by income increases is not immediately neutralized by higher prices, wage increases have the same effect as price wars in the competition for market share: they reduce the difference between unit labor costs and the value created by labor, thus reducing profit as the sole reason for capitalist production.

At the latest in the crisis, when the use of the means of production is no longer worthwhile for many owners of the means of production, the proponents of a supply-oriented policy gain ground by promoting the insight: "Better a low wage than no work". The supply policies advocated by many proponents of capitalism as a reaction to the failure of demand-oriented policies then resolve the contradiction of capitalist production from the other side. Caught up in the rationality of the capitalist mode of production, unemployment in the economic policy debate is suddenly no longer the result of too little demand, but of too high wage costs. *The reduction of unit labor costs becomes the decisive means in the competition for existing purchasing power.*

In a market economy, production takes place only if it is profitable for the entrepreneurs. Because of the failure of demand policy measures, this consequence of capitalist ownership, which is accepted as an economic matter, leads to the conviction that only the improvement of the business conditions of capital can revive the economy.

In the short run, this is a very effective recipe, because just as government stimulus packages stimulate capitalist economic activity before increasingly promoting inflation, the improvement of capitalist business conditions stimulates the growth of the capitalist economy before undermining the necessary purchasing power.

In capitalism – where the living conditions of the population as a cost factor in the profit calculation negatively affects the purpose of production – the dismantling of labor and environmental protection regulations and a drop in wages lead to new business opportunities. However, if these improvements in business conditions are not directly counteracted by import restrictions in the competition among capitalist nations, competition among companies will result in the gradual harmonization of business conditions to a new level. The *"race to the bottom"* initiated by supply policy therefore does not change the fact that the competition for existing purchasing power repeatedly leads to overproduction in relation to purchasing power. At the latest with the crisis - when too much wealth has been created in relation to the population's ability to pay - the proponents of demand-oriented policy gain the upper hand again by pointing to the other side of the contradiction: the purchasing power of the working population as a condition for the profitable use of labor in production.

Better a
low
wage
than no
work

Better a
high
wage
than no
demand

Against the backdrop of stagflation and crisis at the end of the 1970s, and thus the failure of Keynesianism on the one hand, and the escalating national debt under "Reaganomics" on the other, Bill Clinton won the 1992 U.S. presidential election under the label "New Democrats". The economic program with which he took office was an attempt to find a "third way" between classical supply- and demand-oriented economic policy. A few years later in Europe, this program inspired the so-called "New Social Democracy" under Tony Blair and Gerhard Schröder to imitate it.

Under the campaign slogan "Putting People First", Clinton promoted the introduction of mandatory health insurance, increased investment in research and education, and government stimulus programs to promote long-term economic growth while reducing budget deficits. In its first term, the new administration under Bill Clinton initially made some demand-side adjustments to this program, passing tax cuts for the broad middle class while raising the top tax rate to 39.6%. In 1996, under increasing pressure from the Republicans to reduce budget deficits, Bill Clinton announced the end of the era of "big government" and the "welfare state". The ensuing welfare reform, which limited lifetime eligibility to five years, led to a significant reduction in public spending. A total of $260 billion in savings were planned for the 1996 budget, including $125 billion in health care. At the same time, the privatization of public enterprises, which had begun under Reagan, and the deregulation of labor and financial markets were accelerated during Clinton's term.

The positive development of economic indicators initially seemed to confirm the so-called "third way" between supply- and demand-oriented policies. The economic recovery that had already begun under Clinton's predecessor after the economic crisis of 1991 continued and received substantial additional financial resources from the mid-1990s with the boom of the "new economy". Based on the uninterrupted exponential development of microelectronics, new companies were created, financed by massive issuance of new shares in speculation on future profits. From 1993 to the end of 2000, the average growth rate was 4.2%, the unemployment rate fell from 7% to 4%, and the inflation rate averaged less than 3%. Thanks to the tax revenues generated by the economic upswing and the surpluses from the social security funds used to cover the budget, budget surpluses totaling $444 billion have been achieved since 1998. In March 2000, the "third way" ended with the so-called New Economy Crisis.

The "New Economy", financed largely by the issuance of new stock, suffered a massive loss of confidence.

The new administration under G. W. Bush tried to overcome the stock market crash by cutting taxes and interest rates and deregulating the financial markets, thereby creating incentives for renewed speculative money creation. This was intended to stave off the threat of a prolonged economic downturn, and the stimulus measures quickly took effect with an *"economic miracle"* in the construction industry. The enormous extent of the newly unleashed speculation on future income can be well studied in the development of mortgage lending in the U.S.

From $6.5 trillion in 2000, the cumulative volume of mortgage loans rose to $11.5 trillion in 2005 and $14.3 trillion in 2007. A comparison with the growth in gross domestic product shows that U.S. growth during this period was driven primarily by the construction industry. Millions of homes were built in the U.S., and prices rose to the point that more and more people began to buy homes, speculating on the expected increases in real estate prices.

USA

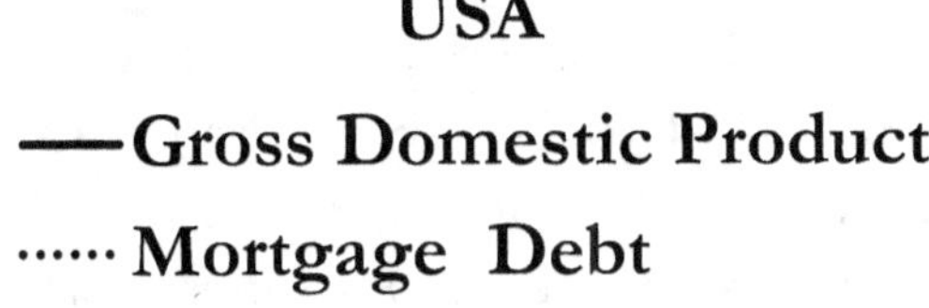

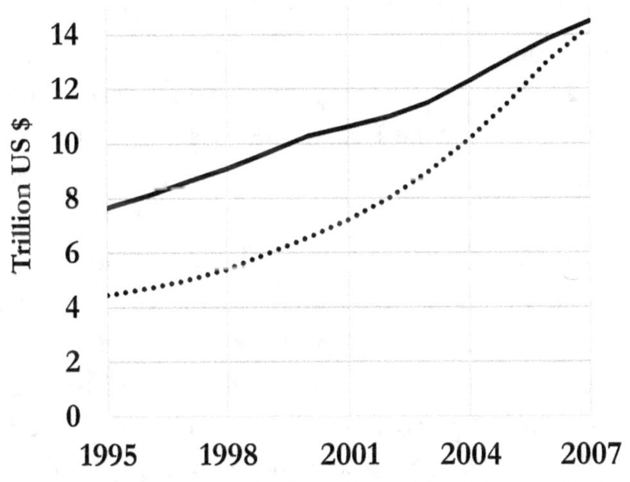

Source: Federal Reserve Economic Data
Mortgage Debt Outstanding, All holders, Annual, Not Seasonally Adjusted

Financing this huge boom in speculation on the future purchasing power of private households, however, required more than just a cut in the Federal Funds Rate from 6.5% to 1%, which the Federal Reserve implemented from 2000 to 2003. By the end of its second term in office, the Clinton administration had already laid the groundwork for the decisive financial innovations that financed the renewed strong economic upswing from 2000 to 2007 with the repeal of the Glass-Steagall Act, a law that separated commercial and investment banks, the Financial Service Modernization Act and the Commodity Futures Modernization Act. A capitalist "economic miracle" in the construction sector, which for several years created real income and consumption opportunities for millions of people that would not have existed within the framework of the capitalist mode of production without the credit expansion made possible by the deregulation of the financial markets. This is a vivid example of how financial capital, through speculation on future incomes, enables all capitalist enterprises, as well as private households, to operate with greater monetary power than they have created themselves.

In order to understand the financial innovation that made it possible to overcome the economic slump that resulted from the "New Economy Crisis" and thus paved the way for a more widespread and massive crisis, it is helpful to first look at how traditional housing market financing works.

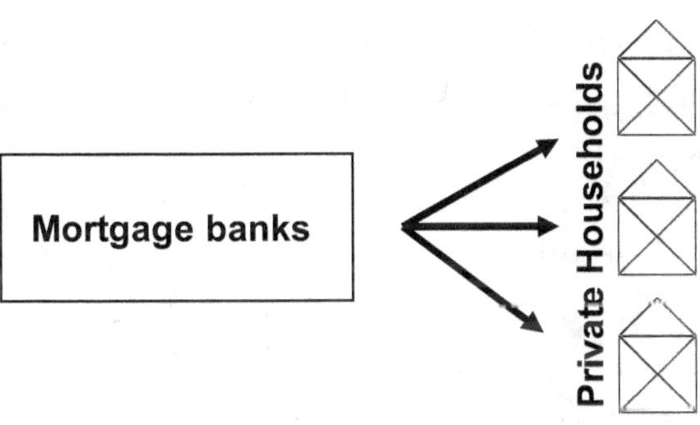

Households obtain the necessary purchasing power to build and buy their own homes through mortgage loans granted by banks speculating on future income against interest. Banks finance their lending activities through their bank deposits or by issuing their stocks and bonds, which they sell to investors on the capital market based on their successful business model. The banks' lending business is essentially limited by their refinancing capacity, i.e. their ability to raise additional equity or debt capital as a basis for their mortgage business.

In order to promote economic growth *beyond the refinancing capacities of the banks*, a so-called secondary market was created in the U.S. via the government-owned and later partially privatized mortgage banks named Freddie Mac and Fannie Mae. In this secondary market, the mortgage banks could sell their mortgage loans and receive almost unlimited funds to make new mortgage loans. The public or semi-public mortgage banks, in turn, refinanced themselves by securitizing the mortgage loans, i.e. by converting them into asset-backed securities through legal framework agreements. These could then be sold on the global capital market to interested investors (banks, insurance companies, pension funds and various public or private investment funds). As a result of the deregulation of the financial markets, investment banks also entered this lucrative business on a large scale. Like the semi-public banks, they bought the mortgage loans from the local mortgage banks to resell them as asset-backed securities to interested investors on the global capital market.

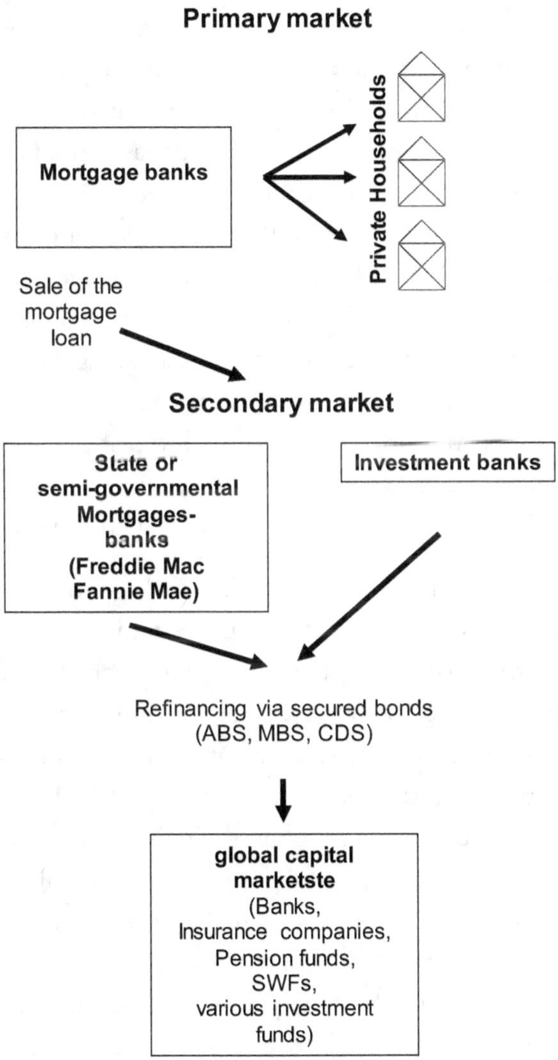

Primary market
Mortgage banks
Private Households
Sale of the mortgage loan
Secondary market
State or semi-governmental Mortgages-banks (Freddie Mac Fannie Mae)
Investment banks
Refinancing via secured bonds (ABS, MBS, CDS)
global capital marketste (Banks, Insurance companies, Pension funds, SWFs, various investment funds)

While the details of asset-backed securities may be complex, the underlying principle is very simple. By transforming mortgage loans into tradable securities, a platform was created on which U.S. banks could effectively lend larger sums of money than would otherwise have been possible on the domestic markets. The legal certainty of the securities' international marketability made it possible to expand mortgage lending through the global capital market. Mortgage lending changed from the sleepy days when mortgage banks held 30-year loans to profit from the difference between their funding costs and the interest paid on the mortgage loans, to a new era where the idea was to resell the loans around the world as quickly as possible.

This pioneering role in the U.S. mortgage market was quickly replicated in other countries and in other sectors of the economy to expand business through credit during the global recovery. In addition to the residential mortgage market, all types of commercial receivables, such as auto leases and consumer debt from the credit card business, were increasingly converted into asset-backed securities and placed on the global capital markets. The extent of the speculation on future business and income that underpinned the capitalist economic boom can be seen by looking at the increase in the ratio of debt to gross domestic product. In the period from 2000 to the peak of the global financial crisis in 2008, total economic debt in the U.S. rose by 64 percentage points, from 180% to 244% of annual economic output. Including financial sector debt, which rose from 41% of GDP at the end of the Clinton era to 57% of GDP in 2008, total U.S. debt rose from 220% to 300% of GDP in eight years.

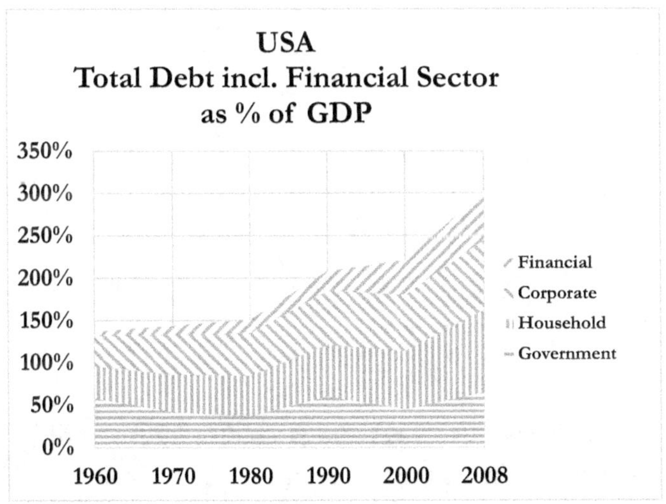

Financial sector debt includes:
• Commercial paper, loans, and bonds issued by banks and other parts of financial sector (e.g., broker-dealers, special-purpose vehicles, insurers)

Financial sector debt excludes:
• Mortgage- and asset-backed securities (e.g., liabilities of Fannie Mae and Freddie Mac in the United States)
• Short-term interbank borrowing
• Retail and corporate deposits, central bank deposits

Source : McKinsey Global Institute, Debt and Deleveraging 2010 / 2013, http://www.mckinsey.com/insights/mgi/research/financial_markets

Over the same period, household debt as a percentage of disposable income reached 125%, up from 89% in 2000.

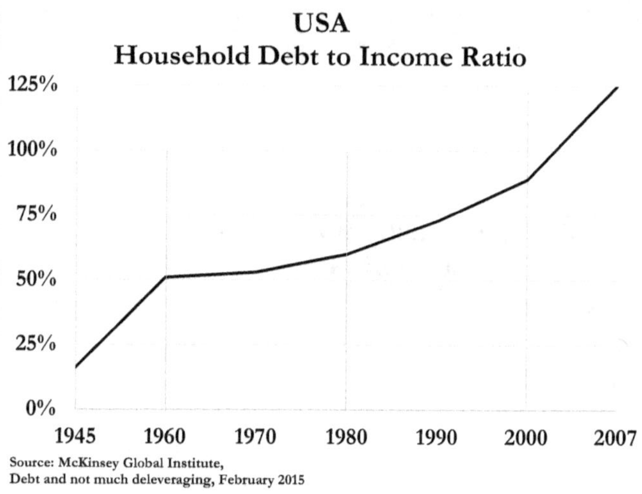

Source: McKinsey Global Institute,
Debt and not much deleveraging, February 2015

On the basis of this expanded credit platform, which was granted in a similar way in European countries, it was possible to produce houses, cars and other consumer goods for seven years after the "New Economy Crisis", speculating on future income. The expansion of credit through the global capital market has provided the capitalist mode of production with the necessary purchasing power to utilize the otherwise idle privatized means of production. A physical wealth that had to be largely destroyed when confidence in credit was lost and everyone suddenly wanted to see money instead of credit.

However, the expansion of credit via the global capital market did not only provide the US and Europe with the necessary solvency required by the capitalist property system to put the otherwise idle privatized means of production into operation. To maintain the value of the U.S. dollar and thus the annual trade deficits, billions of dollars had to be pumped back into the U.S. financial markets. The financing of the U.S. trade deficit through the global sale of asset-backed securities and government bonds since the mid-1990s has made it possible to increasingly relocate production facilities to so-called low-wage countries. In the seven years from 2000 to early 2007 alone, the annual "stimulus package" in countries with which the U.S. had a trade deficit averaged $550 billion.

The global marketing of mortgage-backed securities, which made the gigantic boom in the US housing market possible, thus indirectly financed the purchase of products from so-called low-wage countries. In particular, the *deficit cycle* with China became the engine of global economic growth: the U.S. economy bought goods in China as part of its trade deficit, and the Chinese state bank invested the dollars from its trade surplus in U.S. Treasury bonds and securitized U.S. mortgage loans.

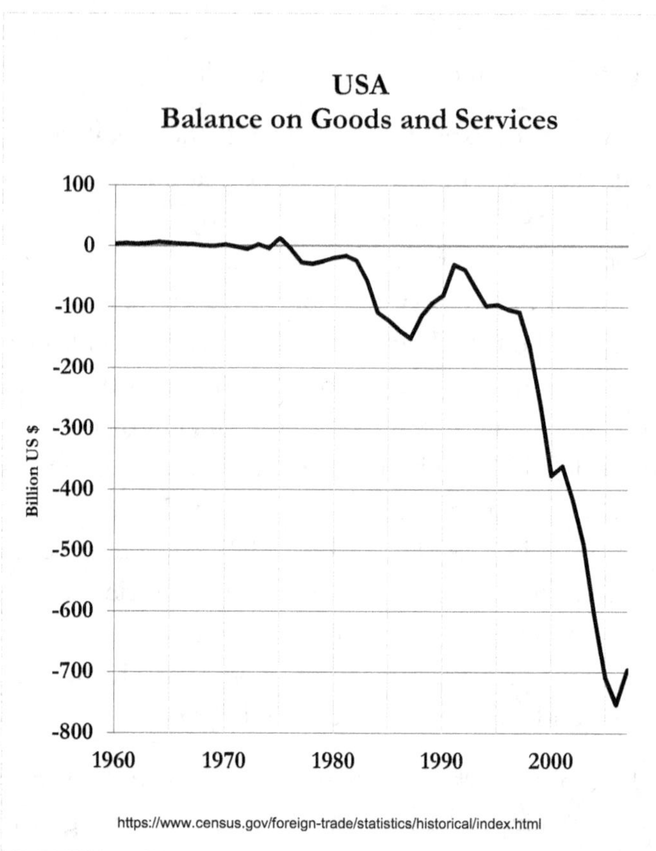

Without the purchasing power generated by U.S. credit, the Chinese "economic miracle" would have simply run out of money. The world's production potential would not have been utilized for lack of solvency. Instead, unemployment and impoverishment, along with overcapacity, would have reached new record levels.

The global financial crisis, like the capitalist crises that preceded it, is therefore neither the consequence of bad economic policy nor the result of irresponsible speculators and greedy bank managers. Without the politically promoted services of finance capital, capitalist production would not have existed on the scale it has in real terms since the industrial revolution. Out of its business interests, finance capital has ensured that the purchasing power necessary for capitalist production has been created in the form of various credit products, ranging from simple bank loans, stocks and bonds to derivative financial instruments.

Capitalist economic crises are not caused by wrong economic policies or the dominance of finance capital, but by the purpose that prevails in capitalism. A purpose that is not simply the communally planned production of useful things to provide for the members of society, but the accumulation of capital. Capital that the private owners of the means of production invest in the expansion and improvement of production processes in competition for market shares, as long as it is foreseeable that the use of labor power promises a profit for the capitalists. With the enormous volume of speculation on future business success made possible worldwide by the technology of securitization, the potential for devaluation increased and developed into a crisis when it was realized that many houses, cars, and the corresponding production capacity and jobs had no prospect of profitability and thus became useless. A little more than 170 years ago, Karl Marx and Friedrich Engels expressed this contradiction of capitalist production as follows:

> *"In these crises, there breaks out an epidemic that, in all earlier epochs, would have seemed an absurdity — the epidemic of over-production. Society suddenly finds itself put back into a state of momentary barbarism; it appears as if a famine, a universal war of devastation, had cut off the supply of every means of subsistence; industry and commerce seem to be destroyed; and why? Because there is too much civilization, too much means of subsistence, too much industry, too much commerce.*
>
> *...*
>
> *And how does the bourgeoisie get over these crises? On the one hand by enforced destruction of a mass of productive forces; on the other, by the conquest of new markets, and by the more thorough exploitation of the old ones. That is to say, by paving the way for more extensive and more destructive crises, and by diminishing the means whereby crises are prevented."* [16]

---

[16] K. Marx and F. Engels, Manifesto of the Communist Party www.marxists.org/archive/marx/works/download/pdf/Manifesto.pdf, p. 17

5. The End of Classical Economic Policy

In August 2007, an epidemic broke out in the leading capitalist nations: The epidemic of overproduction. The economic boom, made possible for seven years by the expansion of credit through the global capital market, reached the point in early 2007 where, with declining confidence in the ability to continue indebtedness, the cost of debt restructuring was rising, leading to increasing defaults. Although in theory there is no exact point at which over-indebtedness is reached, in practice this was the point at which confidence in the ability to service debt declined. Real estate sales on the east and west coasts of the United States began to stagnate and, beginning in 2007, prices began to decline. On August 9, 2007, the interbank market in Europe came to a brief standstill. On September 15, 2008, Lehman Brothers filed for bankruptcy. More and more financial institutions in the U.S. and Europe got into financial difficulties. The whole chain of assets and liabilities that had been built up worldwide in speculation on future income through credit in the form of asset-backed securities broke down, and capitalist production and its financial system were on the verge of collapse. Too much wealth was suddenly accompanied by too little purchasing power.

What until recently had promised to be a successful business suddenly turned out to be "overproduction" in money terms. The financial industry laid off thousands of its employees. The automotive industry found that with the collapse of credit, there was not enough solvency left for a large portion of its cars. Too many cars were being produced, and production capacity was suddenly too large for years. Similar discoveries were made in the engineering and consumer goods industries. Unemployment rose, and with it impoverishment, even though the material wealth of society had not disappeared. It was simply no longer needed for the purposes of the capitalist mode of production.

At the height of the crisis in 2008, total debt including the financial sector in the U.S. and Europe had reached three times the annual economic output. *A default of just 25% of credit-financed economic activity threatened to destroy assets and ultimately solvency equivalent to 75% of annual economic output.*

Total Debt incl. Financial Sector
as % of GDP
2008

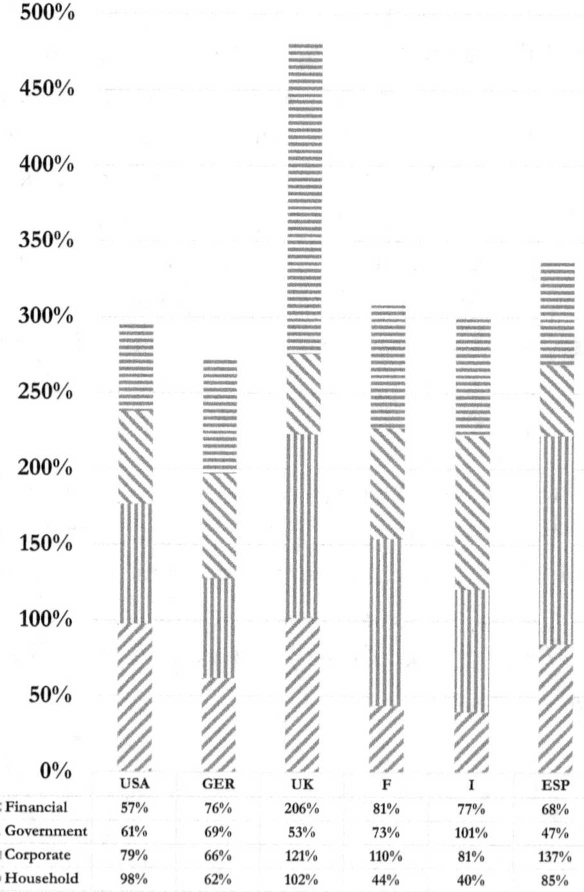

	USA	GER	UK	F	I	ESP
Financial	57%	76%	206%	81%	77%	68%
Government	61%	69%	53%	73%	101%	47%
Corporate	79%	66%	121%	110%	81%	137%
Household	98%	62%	102%	44%	40%	85%

Source : McKinsey Global Institute, Debt and Deleveraging 2010 / 2013,
http://www.mckinsey.com/insights/mgi/research/financial_markets

The coexistence of overcapacity and mass impoverishment, which had taken extreme forms in 1929 in the context of the Great Depression, seemed only a small foretaste of the devastating effects of the crisis that was now looming, given the scale of the impending collapse of the credit chain that had been built up over six decades to fuel capitalist growth. A scenario that had to be prevented by all available means.

In order to maintain capitalist production, insolvent banks and insurance companies had to be propped up by state guarantees. By the end of 2008, some $800 billion had been spent on government bailouts in the U.S. and €1.6 trillion in the EU. In parallel with the bailouts of non-performing loans, a policy of low interest rates, similar to the one introduced after the "New Economy Crisis", has been introduced to revive lending in the capitalist economy, speculating on *future* earnings.

The economic downturn that began in the context of the global financial crisis also led to an increase in government budget deficits due to tax shortfalls and a sharp rise in social security spending. Social security spending rose from 2.9% to 13.2% of GDP in the United States, from 3.0% to 10.8% in the United Kingdom, from 0.3% to 3.0% in Germany, from 2.5%

to 7.1% in France, from 1.5% to 5.3% in Italy, and from 2.0% to 11.0% in Spain.[17]

From 2007 to 2019 (before the impact of the Corona crisis), the ratio of government debt to economic output in the U.S. and most European countries reached levels significantly higher than before the global financial crisis. Government spending, sustained by additional borrowing in the context of budget deficits, thus prevented a much larger reduction in productive capacity due to a lack of purchasing power.

---

[17] International Monetary Fund, World Economic Outlook Database, October 2015

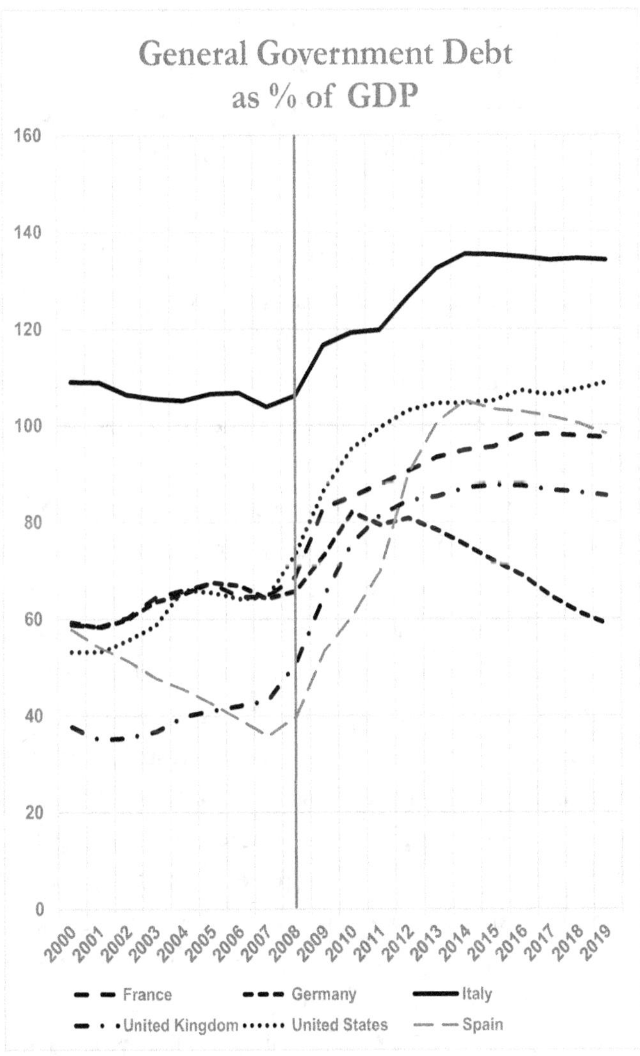

Source: IMF Data Mapper
www.imf.org/external/datamapper/GG_DEBT_GDP@GDD/USA/DEU/FRA/ITA/GBR

Instead of forecasting the further development of debt in the U.S. and Europe, the example of Japan can be used to study where the evolving contradiction of capitalist production and the economic policy attempts to cope with it have already led.

Japan had its "great financial crisis" in the early 1990s. Before that, Japan was known as an economic miracle, similar to China today. The collapse of the real estate and stock markets alone wiped out three times the country's 1989 GDP. In 1929, when the Great Depression wiped out assets equal to the U.S. gross domestic product, the country's economic output fell by 46 percent. When assets equivalent to three times Japan's GDP were devalued, Japan's economic collapse should have been much more severe. However, the Japanese government was able to avert the imminent collapse of the Japanese banking system, the wave of bankruptcies in the real economy, and the threat of mass unemployment through massive government spending programs. Whereas in 1990, at the end of the boom, the corporate sector still accounted for the largest share of debt, in response to the crisis, the government took on the bulk of Japan's debt as a result of the sharp rise in budget deficits to save the economy from a devastating collapse. Ten years after the crisis, public debt rose from 89% to 167%, reaching 228% in 2010, and a new peak of 259% of annual economic output in 2020. Japan's total debt reached four times gross domestic product in 2020.

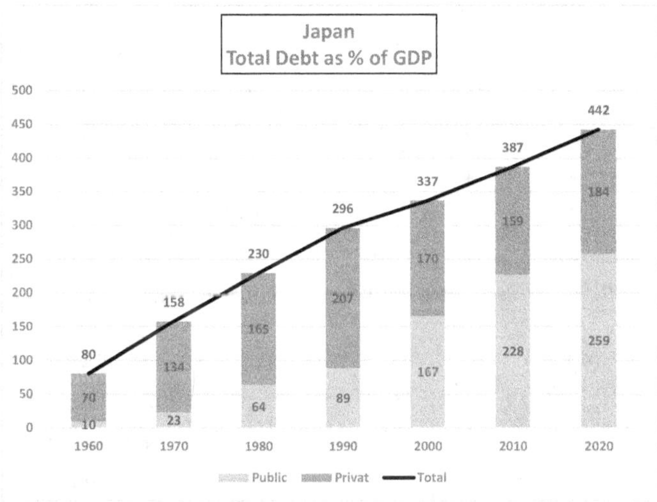

Source : Global Debt Monitor https://www.imf.org/en/Publications

For more than 30 years, successive governments in Japan have tried to overcome economic stagnation through policies of low interest rates and fiscal stimulus. The lack of success is reflected in the fact that despite historically low interest rates, debt servicing already consumes 40% of the government's annual tax revenue, while the debt burden continues to rise. As a result, any significant rise in interest rates threatens to have a devastating impact on the country's finances. In this situation, the attempt by central banks in the U.S. and Europe to end loose monetary policy in the face of the inflation it is fostering puts the Bank of Japan in a very difficult position where it faces the following dilemma: It has to choose between defending the national currency, i.e. fighting inflation, and ensuring solvency. In other words: between ending quantitative easing in order to prevent a further depreciation of the yen and thus an increase in inflation, and maintaining quantitative easing in order to avoid over-indebtedness of the economy and public finances.

Against the backdrop of the sharp rise in public debt in the U.S., Europe and Japan in the wake of the crisis and the simultaneous lack of success in promoting growth, the creditworthiness of even the largest capitalist economic powers can no longer be taken for granted. When assessing the creditworthiness of government finances, rating agencies and investors interested in government bonds are less concerned with the absolute amount of government-guaranteed debt or a specific ratio to economic output. It is the trend in the now historically high relative debt burden, which has been negative for years, that is decisive for the necessary confidence in the government's creditworthiness. As this development continues, it can no longer be ruled out that some of the largest capitalist states in terms of GDP will become insolvent as a result of the debt required to maintain capitalist business. This is a scenario in which the global capitalist financial system would be affected due to the close interconnectedness of credit chains on the international capital markets, in contrast to previous sovereign debt crises that only affected individual countries.

Because of their rising debt burden in relation to economic output, the leading capitalist nations are therefore increasingly facing the same economic policy dilemma that has been observed in the past in the so-called developing and emerging countries. All measures to reduce public debt, whether through tax increases or spending cuts, are proving to be extremely contradictory without economic growth.

A return to top income tax rates of 70%, as in the U.S. in the 1970s, would be conceivable. But why should the same policies that were abandoned during periods of stagflation in the face of high unemployment and inflation serve capitalist growth this time? The obvious idea that it would be possible to deprive the rich of part of their vast fortunes by means of a wealth tax in order to restructure the budget is quickly confronted with the fact that a large part of their assets is used as share capital in capitalist economic life. A forced sale of these assets as part of higher taxes would not only lead to a devaluation of the assets, but also to a withdrawal of the capital resources needed for capitalist growth. The purpose of promoting the capitalist economy would be reversed by the withdrawal of this capital. *The contradiction of capitalist production cannot be overcome by redistributing income.* Fiscal policy does not change the cause of falling growth rates. By reducing the value of products and laying off superfluous labor, the competing measures to increase capital growth simultaneously limit it.

Reducing the expenditure side as a measure of fiscal consolidation is a similarly contradictory instrument because of the weak growth that needs to be overcome. Since reducing budget deficits through spending cuts takes purchasing power away from the economy, radical spending reduction programs are subject to strict limits. *Without economic growth, it is counterproductive to reduce the debt incurred to stimulate growth.* In this situation, therefore, it is not the withdrawal but the injection of money that is necessary, both for the capitalist economy and for the strained government budget. However, the classical Keynesian policy of drastically increasing public spending until the private sector is able to support the economic upswing again lacks the necessary persuasive power in scientific and political circles due to the already historically high level of public debt. In addition to individual government stimulus packages, monetary policy measures should therefore provide the necessary liquidity. On the one hand, state guarantees ensure that the bursting of credit claims in the course of the financial crisis does not lead to widespread bankruptcies in the banking sector; on the other hand, a policy of low or even negative interest rates should encourage the creation of money, which is essential for the capitalist economy. Supporting bad loans with state guarantees and promoting new loans is the contradictory economic policy aimed at preventing the impending global economic crisis.

Faced with low growth rates, the governments and their central banks in the three major capitalist centers have made the fight against deflation their top priority in order to break the impending vicious circle of falling creditworthiness with rising interest rates, a corresponding further increase in public debt and a subsequent fall in creditworthiness. The spectre of deflation is supposedly being raised. But what is so devastating about falling prices for goods and services? Customers like it, and so do the purchasing departments of large corporations. By relocating production to low-wage countries, the capitalists themselves ensure that wages are lowered and that the cost advantage is ultimately reflected in lower prices through market competition, the desired principle of the market economy. The same is true of productivity progress, which reduces costs and lowers prices through competition. But it is precisely this contradiction of capitalist production that is the reason for the specter of deflation: the greater the productivity, the less labor time is needed to produce a commodity, the lower the value of the commodity, which is the only thing that matters in capitalist production.

As explained in the previous chapter, this contradiction can theoretically take two opposite forms: growth that compensates or even overcompensates for the loss of value, or rising unemployment. In the past, the fundamental inventions during the first and second industrial revolutions enabled the expansion of new markets for several decades, more than compensating for the displacement of traditional markets. From household appliances and consumer electronics to transportation technology, medical care, and large parts of the food industry, extensive additional product areas were created over and above the increase in productivity of existing production processes. Already at the end of this market expansion made possible by technological leaps, the capitalist centers were confronted with declining growth rates, which could not be prevented even by increasing relative indebtedness to maintain solvency. With the third industrial revolution - the development of microelectronics and the extensive possibilities for automation it has created - the challenge of overcoming the contradiction of capitalist production is further intensified. Although new and expanded product fields will emerge in the context of this renewed accelerated technological development, they will by no means be on the scale of the first and second industrial revolutions. The self-driving car will come, but in terms of market expansion it will be insignificant compared to the original replacement of the horse-drawn carriage by the internal combustion engine. The same is true of the radio, the gramophone, and the television, which contributed more to market expansion than the new technologies of the last two decades. The main difference in the new technological leap is that, instead of expanding the market, the productivity of existing production areas is increased, so that the new products, in relation to the number of units, require significantly fewer workers from the outset than was the case when new markets were created in the wake of the first and second industrial revolutions.

United States
GDP growth rate

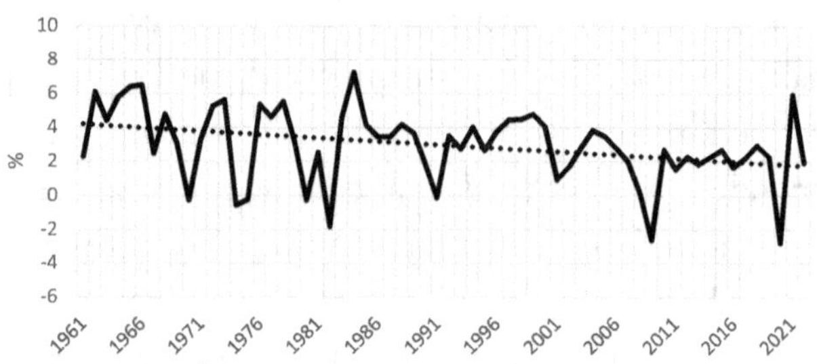

Japan
GDP growth rate

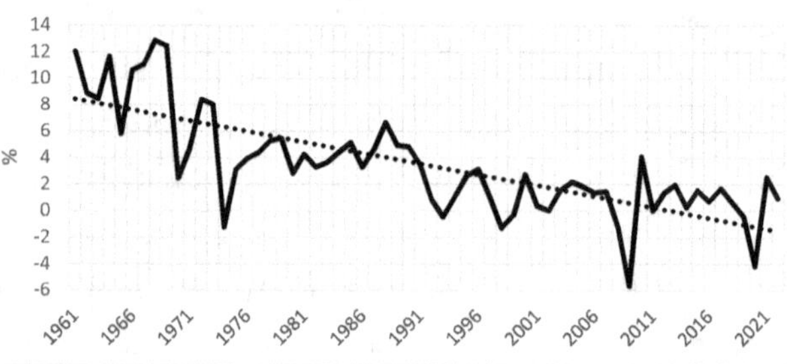

Euro area
GDP growth rate

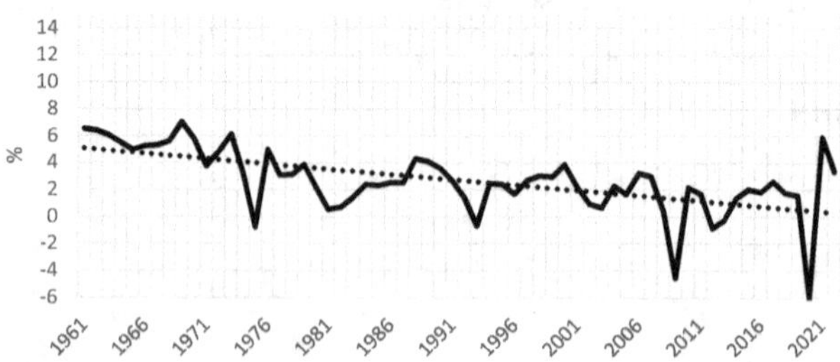

Source: World Bank Data,
https://data.worldbank.org/indicator/NY.GDP.MKTP.KD.ZG?locations=JP-US-XC

The reduction of value and solvency as a result of the contradiction of capitalist production - the effort to reduce labor time to a minimum, while at the same time it is the measure and source of capitalist wealth - requires overcompensating growth, whether through new fields of production or new markets. If the purchasing power of the population in the developing and emerging countries were to increase significantly in the coming years, additional markets would emerge that would be larger than those in the already developed capitalist countries. With the development of the Asian "tigers" in the 1970s and 1980s, the opening up of the former Eastern bloc countries in the early 1990s and the increasing expansion of capitalist markets to the BRICS countries, the share of the developing and emerging countries in the world's gross domestic product has already risen from 37% to 60% between 1980 and 2020. However, almost ninety percent of this growth was due to the development of the People's Republic of China alone.[18]

The extent to which developments similar to China's are possible in other previously capitalistically under-developed markets, or whether the relocation of pro-duction to so-called low-wage countries has already been largely completed without a sustained increase in domestic demand in these countries, cannot be clearly

---

[18] I M F, World Economic Outlook Database, April 2020

answered at present. Even the question of whether China's crucial transformation from a "low-wage country" to a developed capitalist economy will succeed or fail will ultimately be decided by the competition in the market between corporations and the nations that support them.

But market competition is only one side of the coin. The contradiction of capitalist production driven by competition also plays an essential role in the fundamental question of the possibility of developing additional markets. Even in the "low-wage countries", workers are now increasingly facing competition from industrial robots. For example, while the U.S. textile industry was largely outsourced to countries like China, India and Mexico in the 1990s, there have been signs of a trend reversal in recent years. Already in 2013, the New York Times reported under the title "U.S. Textile Plants Return, With Floors Largely Empty of People" that between 2009 and 2012, U.S. textile exports rose by 37 percent to a total of $23 billion.[19] According to a survey by the Boston Consulting Group, half of U.S. manufacturing companies with revenues of more than $10 billion are now actively considering moving factories back to the United

----

[19] www.nytimes.com/2013/09/20/business/us-textile-factories-return.html?pagewanted=all&_r=

States.[20] A trend reversal made possible by automation technology, which can now be used to compete with low wages abroad.[21] But even in the "low-wage countries," advancing automation technology is increasingly becoming a worthwhile investment. According to a study by the International Federation of Robotics, China is already the largest buyer of industrial robots.[22] A prime example of this technological evolution is Foxconn, one of the world's largest manufacturers of electronics and computer parts, which employed 900,000 people in its Chinese factories in 2014. By investing in automated production facilities, the company plans to reduce its workforce to 550,000 by 2023.[23]

Another not insignificant aspect in the question of whether the additional markets necessary for capitalist

---

[20] Martin Ford, The Rise of the Robots. Technology and the Thread of Mass Unemployment, Oneworld Publications, 2015
[21] See for example: Martin Wolf, Why the Techno-optimists are wrong, in: The Fourth Industrial Revolution. A Davos Reader, Council on Foreign Relations 2016
[22] http://www.ifr.org/news/ifr-press-release/industrial-robots-post-a-new-sales-record-in-2015-806/
[23] https://de.wikipedia.org/wiki/Foxconn
The demographic effects, which in the case of China counteract the effect of automation, are not considered here, as the assessment of the prospects of success of China's transformation is not the subject of this book. A good presentation of this can be found in: Richard C. Koo, The Escape from Balance Sheet Recession and the QE Trap

growth will develop is that the emerging "export nations" themselves depend to a considerable extent on
the solvency of the leading capitalist economic powers. Without their capital transfers, as well as their im-
ports, the "low-wage countries" will lose the purchasing power from their exports, which in turn is the pre-
requisite for the compensatory growth of capital in the
developed countries. When China's export industry
was hit by the collapse of solvency in the U.S. and Europe in the course of the global financial crisis, the
Chinese government immediately responded with
massive state investment programs and the promotion
of a general credit policy. "While many pundits both
inside and outside the country are criticizing the government for building wasteful, inefficient projects",
writes Richard C. Koo, chief economist at the Nomura
Research Institute in Tokyo, "most of these were public works projects designed to preserve the 60 million
jobs that would have been lost as a result of the global
financial crisis, which originated in the West."[24]

As a result, China's total debt, which at 158% of economic output in 2007 was on par with other developing countries, rose rapidly to 211% by 2010 and
reached 269% in 2020. The sharp rise in the ratio of

---

[24] Richard C. Koo, The Escape from Balance Sheet Recession
and the QE Trap, Wiley 2014, Pos. 6502

total debt to economic output, coupled with a simultaneous decline in the growth rate, is thus also an expression in the case of China of the fact that the Chinese "economic miracle" would have long since run out of money without the increasing speculation on future purchasing power made possible by credit. The development is comparable to the "economic miracle" in Japan from 1960 until the Japanese crisis in 1990.

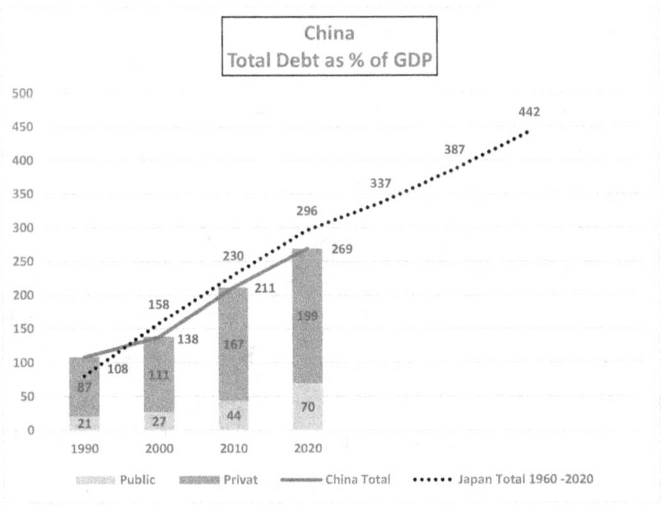

Source : Global Debt Monitor 2023 https://www.imf.org/en/Publications

As can be seen from the example of China's development, the potential for expansion into previously capitalistically underdeveloped markets stands and falls
with the solvency of the leading capitalist economies.
But this is exactly where the evolving contradiction of
capitalist production is buried under the growing debt:
The leading capitalist economic powers hope for the
growing solvency of the new markets, even if it is with
the help of credit, in order to prevent their insolvency,
which has already been postponed by extensive credit.

If the hope of neutralizing the contradiction of capitalist production by expanding the markets does not
work, i.e. if the so-called deflation continues, the debt
ratio will continue to rise inexorably on the basis of
unchanged expenditures. Without economic growth
that more than compensates for the value-destroying
effect of productivity increases, politicians in the leading capitalist economies are thus faced with a contradictory economic policy choice: in the face of weak
growth and over-indebtedness, they must further reduce society's ability to pay through austerity measures
or ensure additional purchasing power through a policy of low interest rates and government spending programs with increased debt.

Faced with this economic policy dilemma, the governments of the leading capitalist nations, together with
their central banks, have decided in 2008 to break a

taboo and promote additional lending. In the context of a policy of extremely low interest rates, they themselves began to buy up government and corporate bonds and asset-backed securities on a large scale under the title of quantitative or monetary easing. With the onset of the global financial crisis, the central banks of the United States, the United Kingdom, the European Union, and Japan tripled the monetary base from about $3 trillion to almost $9 trillion by the end of 2012. In late 2014, the Japanese government announced that it would increase its annual bond-buying program to ¥80 trillion ($0.7 trillion) and continue until inflation reaches two percent. By 2018, the Bank of Japan's balance sheet expansion through this program exceeded the size of Japan's annual economic output. In early 2015, the ECB announced a similar, initially temporary, €0.7 trillion annual program to purchase government and corporate bonds. To avoid a "credit crunch," the program was extended several times, with the ECB's balance sheet total reaching 40% of eurozone GDP in 2017. In contrast, the FED ended its purchase program at the end of 2014 and began to cautiously reduce its balance sheet. However, after interest rates in the US repo market spiked in September 2019, similar to the beginning of the global financial crisis, the FED was forced to change course again in order to avoid a liquidity squeeze in the money market, which is important for the short-term refinancing of banks. In a matter of days, the Federal Reserve made more than $700 billion available to banks.

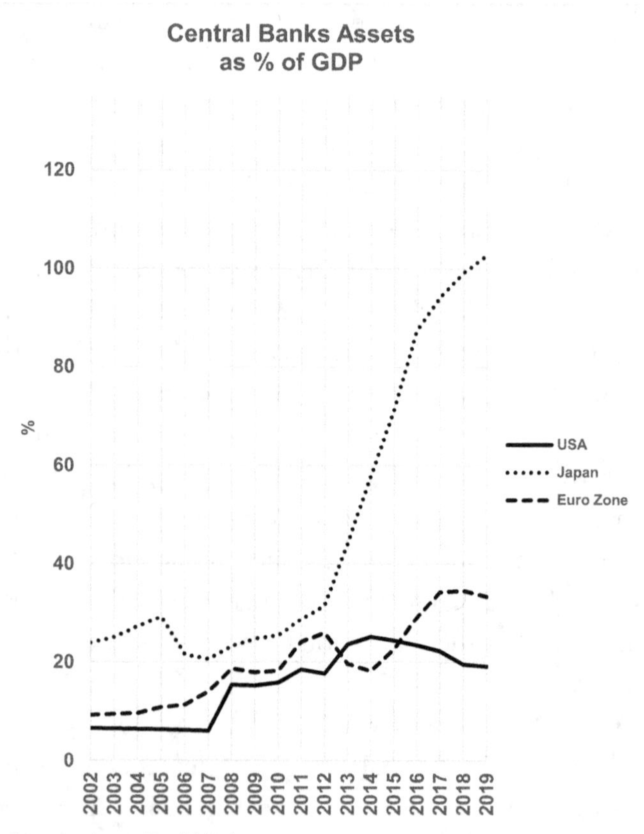

By intervening in the market as bond buyers with money they have created, central banks help to keep nominal interest rates low by increasing the central bank money supply and at the same time provide incentives for additional lending by refinancing loans to credit institutions. The challenge in this balancing act is to slightly increase inflation in the course of a credit-financed economic upswing without raising interest rates and thus the debt burden. By combining low borrowing costs with controlled inflation, central banks aim to contribute to higher growth rates and thus to debt relief for the government and the economy.

However, there is no direct link between central bank money supply and economic growth or inflation. As long as companies and private households are heavily indebted as a result of a previous crisis and debt reduction is therefore a priority for large parts of the economy in order to avoid the threat of insolvency, the way to bring additional solvency into circulation via credit remains blocked. Whether, to what extent and in which economic segments the bank reserves that have grown with the monetary base lead to an increase in lending cannot be controlled by the central banks. Even free credit only leads to an increase in the amount of money in circulation, which in turn opens up scope for production expansion, if potential credit demanders can foresee additional business opportunities and the banks classify their customers as creditworthy. The spectre of deflation, which has its decisive driving force in the contradictions of capitalist production, cannot simply be banished by a "zero interest rate policy" and the inflation of the monetary base by the central banks.[25]

On the contrary, the longer the monetary easing program is used to increase the monetary base by buying up its own government bonds and asset-backed securities from the economy, the greater the likelihood that this will promote new, extensive speculative bubbles in individual sectors of the economy. Instead of promoting economic growth as intended, the lower yields on government bonds resulting from the monetary easing program make the speculative investment of financial capital in riskier assets more attractive. The rising prices of, for example, stocks or real estate, which increase with the additional demand, provide a basis for speculation and thus encourage further inflows of capital seeking investment. As soon as the monetary easing program is reined in, the attractiveness of speculating in alternative assets diminishes with the rising yields on government bonds, and the flow of financial

---

[25] The phenomenon of the so-called "Balance Sheet Recession" was originally described in detail using Japan as an example. Cf. here: Richard C. Koo, The Holy Grail of Macroeconomics. Lessons from Japan's Great Recession, 2009

capital reverses accordingly. The prices of stocks and real estate fall, and the falling prices of bonds with rising interest rates lead to losses in the assets that have been boosted by speculation.[26]

If this leads to a general loss of confidence in speculative value creation, all market participants will want to see money instead of credit. What was recently bought with the prospect of appreciation will now be sold quickly to escape the decline in value. With the collapse of the economic activities stimulated by the monetary easing in the wake of the global financial crisis, governments will then be faced with a *"more extensive and destructive crisis and with diminishing means to prevent the crisis"*, and thus with a dilemma that has become more acute compared to the situation after the global financial crisis. Further borrowing as part of bailouts for the financial sector will further increase public debt and erode already weak sovereign creditworthiness. New rounds of monetary easing will be necessary to prevent the ever more apparent bankruptcy of states, given the otherwise rising interest burden.

---

[26] For details: McKinsey Global Institute, QE and ultra-low interest rates: Distributional effects and risks, 2013 and Richard C. Koo, The Escape from Balance Sheet Recession and the QE Trap. A Hazardous Road for the World Economy, Wiley 2015

At the latest since the historically most extensive global capitalist economic slump to date - which triggered the Corona Pandemic at the beginning of 2020 - there is no longer any sign of a departure from the monetary policy taboo. On the contrary, the amount of liquidity needed to cover bad loans after the global financial crisis pales in comparison to the scale of monetary easing now required to support the global financial system.

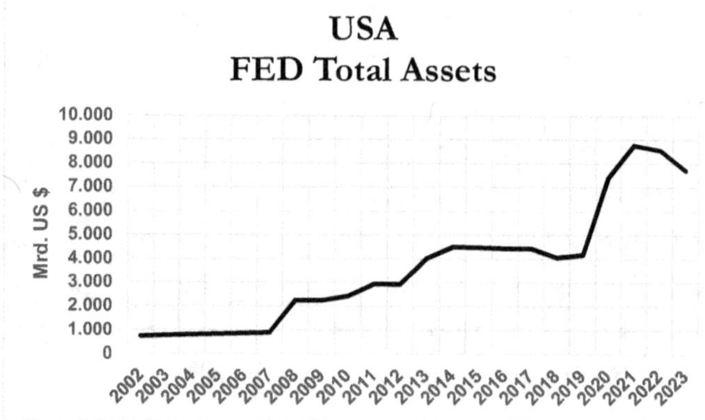

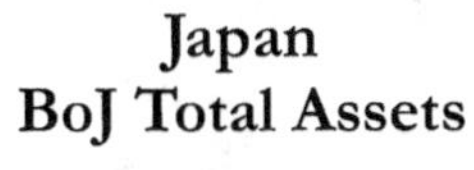

Japan
BoJ Total Assets

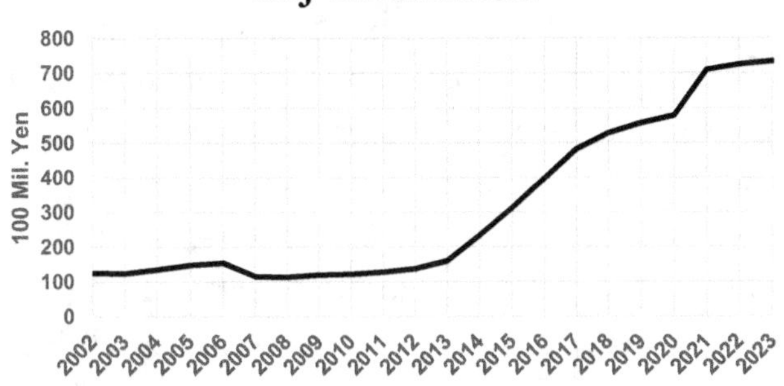

Euro Zone
EZB Total Assets

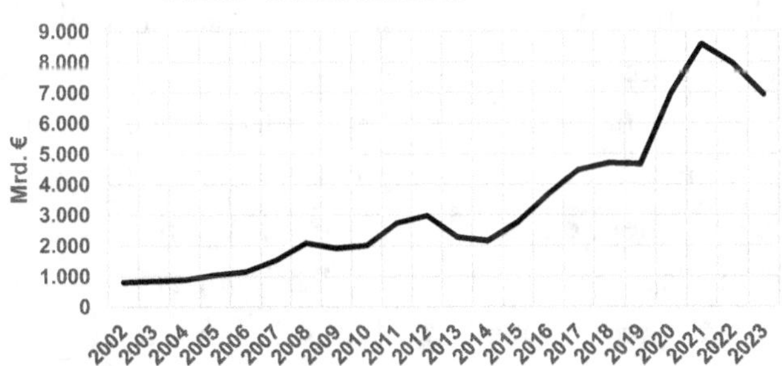

Source: www.tagesgeldvergleich.net

As the monetary easing program in the wake of the 2008 global financial crisis failed to have the desired effect and the "corona crisis" created an urgent need for action, a further break with economic policy taboos was considered. Under the term "helicopter money", originally coined by Milton Friedman, it is being considered whether the desired growth target could not be better achieved directly through the printing press. According to this view, central banks should switch to so-called "monetary financing" (MF), in which the lack of demand is stimulated by the government spending more money and receiving this additional money directly from the central bank without having to repay it. In contrast to the "monetary easing" program, monetary policy expanded into a form of permanent monetary easing could be used to prevent the immanent crash of the financial system and to dispel the "specter of deflation": "The central bank prints money, the treasury distributes it, and the citizens stimulate the economy through additional consumer demand until factory capacities are fully utilized again." [27]

The serious consideration behind this proposal, which at first glance seems absurd, goes back to the so-called "Chicago Plan", a memorandum addressed to US

---

[27] Fear of deflation. The money rain from the helicopter, Frankfurter Allgemeine Zeitung, 22.10.2014

President Roosevelt by a group of economists in 1933 in the wake of the "Great Depression". The core of the proposal, which has been developed by various parties into a reform of the existing monetary order, is the abolition of the banking sector's ability to create credit money in favor of controlled money creation by an independent central bank. Instead of allowing the banking sector to create more than 90% of book money according to its private business interests, the money supply is to be increased or decreased by an independent public money creation committee in a targeted manner with regard to inflation, employment and growth.

> *"If the money creation committee decides to increase the money supply, it simply increases the balance of the central government account at the central bank by the appropriate amount. This non-refundable allocation of new money can be treated by the government as additional revenue that increases its revenue from taxes and debt."* [28]

The additional money can then be circulated by the government according to its economic policy priorities through government spending, tax cuts, repayment of existing government debt, or direct cash transfers to the population. According to this theory, debt-free money would only be inflationary if the

---

[28] A. Jackson, B. Dyson, Modernising Money, Pos. 3824

money supply grew faster than the economy's productive capacity. In the case of underutilization of production capacity, however, the scope for price increases in the short to medium term would be repeatedly eliminated by expanding production in line with the additional ability to pay.[29]

A working paper published by the International Monetary Fund in 2012 assessed the prospects for a fundamental reform of the existing monetary regime along the lines of the Chicago Plan as positive. In line with the study's recommendation, government-controlled money creation that is proportional to GDP growth and largely non-inflationary would not only dampen the ups and downs of the economy, but would also lead to a significant reduction in private and public debt.[30]

However, *the contradictions of capitalist production cannot be resolved by reforming the monetary system.*

---

[29] The concept underlying the Chicago Plan was originally formulated under the leadership of Henry C. Simons and later revised and comprehensively presented by Irving Fisher (Irving Fisher, 100%-Money). Current further developments within the framework of the so-called "New Currency Theory" can be found at Joseph Huber, James Robertson, Creating New Money (2000) and Andrew Jackson, Ben Dyson, Modernising Money (2012)

[30] Jaromir Benes, Michal Kumhof, The Chicago Plan revisited, IWF Working Paper, August 2012

In the market economy, every producer tries to increase his market share in competition with his rivals. No market participant knows whether he or his competitor will be successful. No one knows how much of his products will be needed, whether he will be able to cover his costs, or whether he will be able to sell at all. This contradictory form of social division of labor, in which private producers enter into a social context only after production on the market, is resolved only by success or failure in competition. Behind the backs of the commodity producers, competition decides how and whether private labor proves its value as social labor.

"And how does competition bring about this solution? Simply by depreciating below their labor value those commodities which by their kind or amount are useless for immediate social requirements, and by making the producers feel, through this roundabout means, that they have produced either useless articles or ostensibly useful articles in unusable, superfluous quantity. ... by bringing into operation the law of value of commodity production in a society of producers who exchange their commodities, [the competition] precisely thereby brings about the only organization and arrangement of social production which is possible in the circumstances. Only through the undervaluation or overvaluation of products is it forcibly

brought home to the individual commodity producers what so-ciety requires or does not require and in what amounts." [31]

Therefore, the results of the increase in productivity driven by the competition between nation-states and companies cannot be permanently cancelled out by monetary policy without at the same time calling into question the capitalist mode of production. For example, if the Argentine state were to use monetary policy to permanently compensate for the failure of Argentine companies to compete in world markets, everyone would know that this attempt would not lead to the utilization of Argentine production capacities that are superfluous in the world market, but to the devaluation of the Argentine national credit. No less absurd is the idea that the effects of the successful rationalization efforts of U.S. corporations on the domestic labor market could be avoided by creating money. If companies that are unable to utilize their production capacity due to uncompetitive prices are permanently helped by monetary policy to utilize it, it will be easier for all companies to simply raise prices instead of optimizing production.

---

[31] F. Engels, Preface to Karl Marx: The Poverty of Philosophy
https://www.marxists.org/archive/marx/works/1847/poverty-philosophy/pre-1885.htm
The references in the square brackets were added to the quotation

The discrepancy between claim and reality in the theory of "monetary financing" can be expressed in the words of a representative of the so-called "New Currency Theory" as follows: "The quantity theory of money is a simple and robust piece of economics. It states that an increase in the money supply allows for the realization of economic potential. When such potentials are absent, already realized, or blocked by structural mismatches, more money leads to rising prices." [32]

Because of the contradictions of capitalist production (what they call "structural mismatches"), the capitalist dilemma between unemployment and inflation will not be resolved by state-controlled printing and distribution of money. The credit agreement is linked to the obligation to earn the advance, albeit with a time lag. Because of the growing debt ratio worldwide, and thus the ever less foreseeable ability to fulfill this obligation, abandoning this obligation is not a brilliant idea, but only the last resort to postpone the "Great Depression" of the capitalist mode of production. In this sense, the former head of the British Financial Services Authority, Adair Turner, was already one step closer

---

[32] Joseph Huber, Vollgeld in der Kritik. (The emphasis was added to the quote)

to the truth. In his plea to risk the new monetary order, he wrote under the title *"Between Debt and the Devil"*:

"Monetary finance is like a dangerous medicine, which when taken in small amounts can help cure severe illness but when taken in excess can be fatal. ... the alternative route to nominal demand growth – private credit creation – is just as dangerous." [33]

---

[33] Adair Turner, Between Debt and the Devil: Money, Credit and fixing Global Finance, S.232

"Too much debt, too little growth, and excessively low interest rates," the Bank for International Settlements (BIS), as the central bank of central banks, noted back in 2015 in its annual report on the results of economic policy developments since the global financial crisis, adding as a reminder:

> *"Room for manoeuvre in macroeconomic policy has been narrowing with every passing year. In some jurisdictions, monetary policy is already testing its outer limits, to the point of stretching the boundaries of the unthinkable."* [34]

As these "outer limits" are crossed, the dilemma between reducing debt and increasing credit to stimulate growth is beginning to look like a false choice in the face of low growth rates and rising debt burdens. Indeed, the insolvency threatened by rising debt can theoretically be postponed indefinitely by states using their sovereignty to print and circulate money in order to maintain the capitalist economy.

However, since there is a risk that the intended growth-promoting effect of increasing the money supply would be repeatedly devalued in the course of rising inflation, this attempt would ultimately lead to the same result, which should be avoided by starting the

---

[34] Bank for International Settlements, 85th Annual Report, Basel, 28 June 2015, p. 21

printing press: A currency reform with a corresponding debt reduction, which, with the beginning devaluation of the global credit chain, destroys a large part of society's ability to pay. And since the population excluded from the privatized means of production can only live if it finds work, and can only find work as long as its work increases the capital of the owners of the means of production, a global debt cut with the collapse of the global financial system would directly trigger a world economic crisis. A world economic crisis that differs from the "Great Depression" of the early 20th century in that it is being prepared in the context of globalization as a more extensive and destructive crisis, and that the resources needed to cope with it have already been largely exhausted by the worldwide increase in debt.

When U.S. President Franklin Roosevelt's administration responded to the "Great Depression" in 1933 with the "New Deal", the U.S. national debt was 40 percent of economic output and rose to 52 percent by the end of 1939. Even the Second World War, which Nobel Laureate Paul Krugman considers to have been the decisive debt-financed stimulus to overcome the "Great Depression", only led to a level of public debt that is already being reached at the onset of the current crisis. A simple repeat of the "New Deal" is therefore out of the question. Nor will the enormous market expansion in the course of the Second Industrial Revolution, which brought mass production by means of new materials and production processes and successfully overcompensated for the value- and growth-reducing effect of productivity increases by expanding production in the newly established branches of industry, be repeated in this form. Therefore, the question of whether or after how many years the *"Great Depression 2.0"* can be overcome cannot be answered by referring to the "Great Depression" at the beginning of the last century.

It is absurd.
As more and more products can be
produced with less and less labor,
more and more people are sinking
into a level of poverty
that was unimaginable not long ago.
Even the middle class is now caught
up in the maelstrom of the crisis.

6. The globalized public debt crisis as the highest stage of capitalism?

"The rise of truly intelligent machines, if it comes, would indeed be a big moment in history. It would change many things, including the global economy. Their potential is clear: they would, in principle, make it possible for human beings to live far better lives. Whether they end up doing so depends on how the gains are produced and distributed. It is also possible that the ultimate result might be a tiny minority of huge winners and a vast number of losers. But such an outcome would be a choice, not a destiny. Techno-feudalism is unnecessary. Above all, technology itself does not dictate the outcomes. Economic and political institutions do. If the ones we have do not give the results we want, we will need to change them." [35]

The question of whether capitalism will run out of air in the next great economic crisis due to the evolving contradiction of capitalism can be answered in summary as follows: The air is the money for capitalism, and capitalism will run out of money when not only one state, but the states of the capitalist metropolises as lenders of last resort become insolvent in the collapse of the global financial system. When the insol-

---

[35] Martin Wolf, Why the Techno-optimists Are Wrong, p. 127

vency not only appears as an isolated national debt crisis in the context of competition between nations, but also spreads to a globalized national debt crisis. The mass impoverishment that develops in the capitalist metropolises in the course of the crisis is then no longer the consequence of the perfectly normal capitalist economic cycle, in which an upswing follows the crisis in the short to medium term. Rather, the widespread devaluation of credit shows that the capitalist drive to reduce working hours to a minimum has reached a point of development where, even in the leading industrialized countries, large sections of the population are becoming superfluous to capitalist production.

If this profound devaluation of the capital created by trust in future solvency occurs, the majority of the members of society will be faced with the following fundamental decision due to the unpleasant consequences for them: either they advocate the socialization of the means of production or they adhere to the market economy and thus to the purpose and measure of capitalist production. If they opt for the latter, then sooner or later the many people who are useless for capitalist production will feel the full force of the rationality of the capitalist social order. Welfare state costs for maintaining a functioning army of unemployed people who will no longer be needed in the foreseeable future will quickly be perceived by those who see themselves on the winning side as what they are against the backdrop of the comprehensive devaluation of capital: superfluous costs that capitalist society cannot afford by any stretch of the imagination.

As a result of the deepening global economic crisis, there will then be more and more members of society who demand greater social control of capitalist production relations in line with a *national socialist program*. For as long as the population does not share the arguments against capitalism, their criticism of the increasing impoverishment will not be directed against the purpose of the capitalist mode of production, but against the alleged mistakes and omissions of government representatives. As citizens of a state, they rely on the success of their own nation, which is elevated to the idea of a community. The "prosperity of the nation", which - on the basis of their economic dependence - appears as a condition of their own success , becomes a common need that unites the most diverse social characters into one nation. Belonging to the nation and its progress becomes the highest value for which the willingness to make sacrifices can be demanded. As the hope of participating in national success fades, more and more citizens begin to look for those to blame for the "decline of the nation". Then more and more people organize disobedience against what they see as an incompetent state power because it puts up with too much from other nations or cannot cope with "unnational elements" that are harmful to the community. Then *"the ability and will of the individual to sacrifice for the nation"*[36] become the fundamental forces for the promotion of the *"prosperity of the nation"*.

For this program the antagonism between capital and wage labor need not be abolished. *"The national socialist state has no 'classes'."*[37] It "abolishes" social classes by radically demanding from all its citizens the fulfillment of their duties and the willingness to sacrifice themselves in the service of the nation. This applies both to businessmen, who are ordered to use their private property unconditionally so that the country and its people function as a source of national power, and to workers, who, when they are useless to the business of capital, are promoted to soldiers of labor through state-organized labor services. If, under this program, damage to the economy and the nation is prevented by force, both internally and externally, one thing is made clear at the same time concerning the competition of nations for the riches of the world:

---

[36] Adolf Hitler, Mein Kampf, 102.-106. Edition 1934, p. 167
[37] Adolf Hitler, Mein Kampf, 102.-106. Edition 1934, p. 167

"The talk of the 'economic peaceful' conquest of the world was probably the greatest nonsense ever to be elevated to the guiding principle of state policy ..." [38]

---

[38] Adolf Hitler, Mein Kampf, 102.-106. Edition 1934, p. 158

The *counter-program to capitalism* is to establish a new relationship between the producer and the social product. In order to overcome the existing wage-labor relations, the separation of labor and the product of labor must be abolished, so that the right of disposal over the product of labor, and thus over the means of production, will once again belong to the people.

> *"The workers bring all social functions under their direct administration. They appoint and remove all functionaries. The workers take the social production into their own management by uniting in operational organizations and workers' councils. They themselves switch their operations to the communist economy by calculating their production according to the average social labor time. Thus, the whole society goes over to communist production."* [39]

With the enforcement of individual labor time as the measure of the share in the product of social labor, the transformation from the capitalist to the communist relation of production is completed. The enforcement of individual labor time as the measure of one's share in the product of social labor implies at the same time, the socialization of the means of production by preventing the exploitation of wage labor.

---

[39] Group of International Communists, From each according to his ability, to each according to his needs!, Red & Black Books 2021, p. 28

With the private ownership of the means of production, the exchange of commodities based on private property disappears, and with it the exchange value and its general material form of money. People do everything very simply, without the intermediary of the much-vaunted "value". Instead of valuing individual labor behind people's backs through competition on the markets or through the deliberate regulation of state power in the form of price regulations for goods and labor, people set labor time as the measure of their labor. The communist society is the communal planning of production by free producers on the basis of the calculation of labor time.[40]

---

[40] Presented in detail in: Group of International Communists, Fundamental Principles of Communist Production and Distribution, Red & Black Books 2020

Bibliography

Bank for International Settlements

> 85th Annual Report, Basel, 28 June 2015

Jaromir Benes, Michal Kumhof,

> The Chicago Plan revisited, IWF Working Paper, August 2012

Luigi Buttiglione, Philip R. Lane, Lucrezia Reichlin, Vincent Reinhard

> Deleveraging? What Deleveraging? Geneva Reports on World Economy 16, September 2014

Robert J. Gordon

> The rise and fall of American growth, Princeton University Press 2016

Martin Ford

> The Rise of the Robots. Technology and the Thread of Mass Unemployment, Oneworld Publications, 2015

Michael Heinrich

An Introduction to the Three Volumes of
Karl Marx's Capital, Monthly Review Press
2014

A. Jackson, B. Dyson,

Modernising Money: Why our Monetary System is broken and how it can be fixed, Positive Money 2013

Joseph Huber

Vollgeld in der Kritik. Erläuterungen zum
Vollgeld-Konzept anlässlich Kritik aus verschiedenen ökonomischen Denkrichtungen,
Oktober 2014, S. 20
www.vollgeld.de/vollgeld-in-der-kritik

Richard C. Koo

The Holy Grail of Macroeconomics. Lessons
from Japan's Great Recession,

The Escape from Balance Sheet Recession
and the QE Trap. A Hazardous Road for the
World Economy, Wiley 2015

Paul Krugman

The return of the Depression Economics and
the crisis of 2008, W.W. Norton 2009

End This Depression Now, W. W. Norton 2013

Hermann Lueer

Why hunger? Arguments against the Market, Red & Black Books, 2018

Critique of capitalism and the question of the alternative, Red & Black Books 2020

Fundamental principles of communist production and distribution, Red & Black Books 2018

Karl Marx

Capital Volume 1-3

David McNally

Against the Market. Political Economy, Market Socialism and the Marxist Critique, Verso 1993

Ministry of Finance

Japanese Public Finance Fact Sheet
http://www.mof.go.jp/english/budget/budget/

GegenStandpunkt

    Some remarks about the capitalistic relation
between Work and Wealth https://en.gegen-
standpunkt.com/sites/en.gegenstand-
punkt.com/files/book/gs_work-and-
wealth_1996.pdf

McKinsey Global Institute

    Debt and Deleveraging
2010/11/12/13/14/15

    QE and ultra-low interest rates: Distributional
effects and risks, 2013
  http://www.mckinsey.com/insights/mgi/re-
search/financial_markets

J. Ryan-Collins, T. Greenham, R. Werner, A. Jackson

    Where does Money come from? New Eco-
nomics Foundation 2012

Jeremy Rifkin

    The End of Work. The Decline of the Global
Labor Force and the Dawn of the Post-Market
Era, 1995

Adair Turner

    Between debt and the devil: money, credit
and fixing global Finance, Princeton University Press, 2016

Martin Wolf,
> Why the Techno-optimists are wrong, in: The
> Fourth Industrial Revolution. A Davos
> Reader, Council on Foreign Relations 2016

www.redblackbooks.de

Group of International Communists

FUNDAMENTAL PRINCIPLES OF COMMUNIST PRODUCTION AND DISTRIBUTION

"As simple as the basis for the domination of the working class is, as simple is the *formulation* for the abolition of wage slavery (even if the practical implementation is not so simple!). This abolition can only consist in the abolition of the separation of work and the work product, that the *right of disposal* over the work product and therefore also over the means of production is again given to the workers."

The *»Fundamental Principles of Communist Production and Distribution«* emerged as a reaction to the negative development of the Russian Revolution. With this writing, the authors, for the first time, put up for debate the *economic foundations* for the construction and organization of a society in the sense of the *»association of free and equal people«*. At the same time, they took into account all the experience gained from the previous attempts of the labor movement, and by criticizing it were able to point out necessary new paths. A critique that has lost nothing of its original topicality to this day.

The first edition of the Fundamental Principles, published in German in 1930, was confiscated and largely destroyed. A completely revised and improved edition in Dutch was first published in excerpts in 1931 and 1935 in book form in a second edition. The text of the German first edition was reprinted in 1970 and also translated into English and French. The completely revised and improved 2nd edition, on the other hand, remained largely unnoticed in Dutch for the following 85 years. With this translation of the 2nd edition into English, the Sleeping Beauty has awakened.

GROUP OF
INTERNATIONAL
COMMUNISTS

FROM EACH
ACCORDING TO
HIS ABILITY,
TO EACH
ACCORDING TO
HIS NEEDS!

HERMANN LUEER (ED.)

RED & BLACK BOOKS

GROUP OF
INTERNATIONAL
COMMUNISTS

PUT THE WHOLE
STATE MACHINERY
INTO THE MUSEUM OF
ANTIQUITIES, NEXT TO
THE SPINNING WHEEL
AND THE BRONZE AX!

HERMANN LUEER (ED.)

RED & BLACK BOOKS

Most Marxists do not like Marx. At least, they do not like the economic principles of the communist society that Marx derived from his critique of capitalism. But most Marxists do not criticize Marx in this respect either, they prefer to interpret him.

»Fundamental Principles of Communist Production and Distribution«, the now legendary 1930 pamphlet of the Group of International Communists, was both a detailed exposition of the communist mode of production that Marx and Engels had only sketched out and a fundamental critique of the revisionism of the political parties that invoked Marx.

The books contain a selection of articles published by the members of the Group of International Communists in various periodicals between 1925 and 1936, whose critique has lost none of its relevance the present day.

HERMANN LUEER FUNDAMENTAL PRINCIPLES OF COMMUNIST PRODUCTION AND DISTRIBUTION

RED & BLACK BOOKS

This book is a tribute to the collective work of the Group of International Communists of Holland. Given the experiences with state communism in Russia, their »Fundamental Principles of Communist Production and Distribution«, published in 1930, was an attempt to elaborate the economic basis of a communist society as outlined by Karl Marx and Friedrich Engels. Although their explanations have lost none of their original topicality, their text has remained a product of its time in the way they address the literature of that period. This paper, therefore, attempts to reintroduce the core statements of the »Fundamental Principles of Communist Production and Distribution« into the current debate on alternatives to capitalism.

HERMANN LUEER
WHY HUNGER?
ARGUMENTS AGAINST THE MARKET
RED & BLACK BOOKS

HERMANN LUEER
CRITIQUE OF CAPITALISM
AND THE QUESTION OF THE ALTERNATIVE
RED & BLACK BOOKS

Mistakes in explaining the cause of a disturbing effect usually lead to the wrong proposed solution. Those who explain poverty as the result of market failure seek alternatives to market regulation. Those who explain poverty as a necessary consequence of the market economy want to abolish the market. Any alternative to capitalism is therefore only as good as the underlying explanation of the capitalist mode of production to which it is supposed to be an alternative. Accordingly, this book is not about imagining a better world, regardless of the reasons for the worldwide impoverishment and misery of large sections of the population, but about deriving from the explanation of capitalism the fundamental principles of an economy beyond capitalism. Critique and alternative are thus brought together. The question of feasibility is thus resolved of itself.

www.ingramcontent.com/pod-product-compliance
Lightning Source LLC
Chambersburg PA
CBHW070841250726
48662CB00003B/1319